OUR CUMBRIA

THE STORIES OF CUMBRIAN MEN AND WOMEN

Cover Illustrations:

Top left: Hilda Foster. *(Chapter 3. Farmer's Wife)*

Top right: Percy Duff, a well known figure, formerly Borough Chamberlain of Kendal. *(Chapter 17. Town Treasurer)*

Bottom left: Arthur Pickthall, age 97, a Cumbrian farmer who carried stones to direct his sheep on the fells when he couldn't afford a dog. *(Chapter 23. Ninety-seven Years of Farming)*

Bottom right: Jim Dixon, who spent many years at Stott Park Bobbin Mill. *(Chapter 2. Working with Bobbins)*

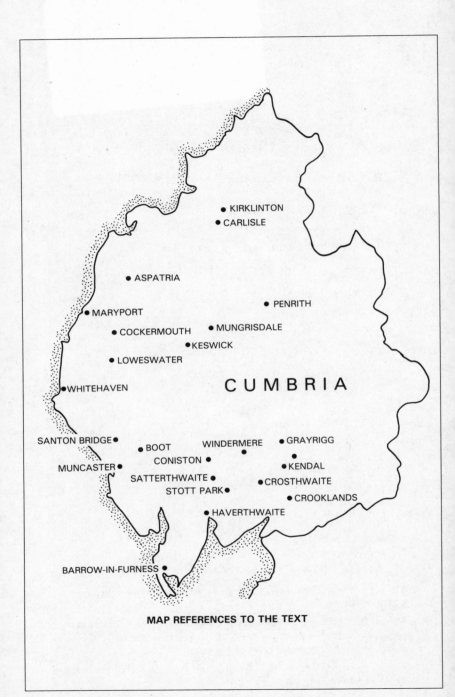

KIRKLINTON
CARLISLE

ASPATRIA

PENRITH

MARYPORT

COCKERMOUTH   MUNGRISDALE

KESWICK

LOWESWATER

WHITEHAVEN

CUMBRIA

SANTON BRIDGE   WINDERMERE   GRAYRIGG

BOOT
CONISTON   KENDAL

MUNCASTER

SATTERTHWAITE   CROSTHWAITE
STOTT PARK

CROOKLANDS

HAVERTHWAITE

BARROW-IN-FURNESS

MAP REFERENCES TO THE TEXT

OUR CUMBRIA

THE STORIES OF
CUMBRIAN MEN AND WOMEN

Recorded by JACK GILLESPIE

CICERONE PRESS

MILNTHORPE, CUMBRIA

ISBN 1 85284 035 8
© *Jack Gillespie 1989*

First Published 1989

Dedication
*For Susie, Morag and Andrew
who enriched my life.*

Acknowledgement

Many thanks are due to the following for allowing
me to use their photographs: Margaret Duff Collection,
Leslie Leak, J. and E. Forder, Ivor Nicholas, Carr's of
Carlisle, Whitehaven Museum, British Coal, Barrow-
in-Furness Library, Gawith Hoggarth and Co. Ltd., K.
Shoes, Cumbria Constabulary, Westmorland Gazette,
Ray Bishop, W.Guest, V.S.E.L. (Vickers Shipbuilders),
British Nuclear Fuels Ltd., James Cropper Plc.,
R.Sanderson, E.Bowness.

Printed and bound in Great Britain by
Butler & Tanner Ltd, Frome and London

CONTENTS

Introduction

"My life has been very ordinary. I haven't much to tell." This is the reaction of most old people who undervalue their experiences. Because their stories are unrecorded, much social history is lost forever.

In Cumbria as elsewhere this is unfortunately true; made more regretful because the rate of change has accelerated during the last fifty years. In Cumbria there is a rich agricultural, industrial and cultural web of heritage woven from the workaday lives and characters of ordinary folk.

I have tried to do two things. One is to capture the simple but absorbing stories of peoples' lives. The other is to preserve for future generations of Cumbrians elements of social and environmental change in the early and middle years of the 20th century.

As a token of respect for the older generation all royalties from this book go to Age Concern.

TOM BARBOUR

A Bobby's Life in Cumbria

"I am now in my late-eighties and have worked all my life in Cumbria.

"The men on night duty were assembled in the charge room at Whitehaven Police Station on a cold November evening in 1926. They comprised an inspector, sergeant and seven constables. The inspector called 'Fall in'. The constables formed a line. They varied in age and service. I was the junior.

"The inspector, reading from a slate, called out the number of one of six beats each man would work, also the time of his half-hour break for refreshment. We brought our own refreshments and deposited them on a shelf. Handcuffs and batons were produced for inspection, but never our torches, which I considered strange as they were so essential on night duty. We had been issued with the bull's eye oil burners which the older men said were good hand-warmers, even if they did occasionally smoke, but we preferred the electric torches, which we bought instead.

"The seventh constable would remain in the charge room on reserve. He had to attend to the telephone as the office closed at 10.00 a.m.. He would search any 'arrests' before putting them in the cells, where he would visit them regularly.

"The inspector read, from a typed sheet, the addresses of all private houses where the occupants had reported they would be away from home. Each man had to check those on his beat. At 9.55 p.m. we marched out in single file, passing the men on the afternoon shift who were lined up waiting to enter the charge room at 10.00 a.m. to be dismissed. Three eight hour periods were worked, every eighth being an individual's rest day.

"The charge room was a relic of the Victorian era. It was a large, oblong, cheerless room with three windows which looked onto a yard and high wall. In front of the windows was a high-sloping Dickensian desk with three lids under which were charge books and foolscap for reports. All reports were written here, sitting on high, uncomfortable stools. There was a fire and wooden bench on which the constables could sit when having their refreshment.

7

"Whitehaven was a busy, compact seaport and market town with 18,000 inhabitants. There were three collieries on the perimeter which provided the bulk of employment. The coal was mostly shipped to Ireland. Work in the loading dock was continuous day and night. The town lay in a hollow and all roads leading from it were steep.

"Five of the beats each comprised several streets. The doors of all shops and business premises were checked by anyone on night duty. Any doors that were insecure, usually in consequence of neglect when closing, were dealt with in a prescribed manner. The sixth beat, on the outskirts of the town, was mostly residential.

"On each beat were points where a constable had to be at pre-scribed times in order that the supervising officer could meet him. These points would be a street corner, public building or a shop. The places and times were changed to prevent them becoming public knowledge.

"The beat system was designed to present an element of surprise, but apart from petty thefts, serious crime was conspicuous by its rarity. Police had authority which was recognised by the public and supported by the courts. A fine imposed by magistrates invariably had an alternative prison sentence in the event of the fine not being paid. The latter would be served in a county jail, which meant strict discipline and few privileges. They were intended to be places of correction. The prospect of being sent there had a deterring influence. Children were afraid of policemen, in consequence no doubt of parents threatening to bring one to a child who misbehaved. Traffic caused no problems, there being few accidents. The number of registered motor vehicles in the whole country was under a million.

"I had been a tenant of a small farm for three years when unem-ployment began to increase and shortly was followed by the Depres-sion. There were no subsidies or assistance of any kind for farmers. Those who owned their farms or had been long established could weather the crisis, even while feeling the pinch. Those situated as I was, found the prospect was bleak. Deciding to change my occupa-tion, until normal conditions in agriculture returned, I joined the Cumberland and Westmorland Constabulary.

"Along with two other recruits I commenced a three month training course, based in a room at Penrith Police Station. The chief constable's office was on the first floor. In January 1926, when our training was over - with no examination - the three of us were posted to Whitehaven, aware that our training had failed to provide any-

sergeant instructor was an ex-naval man.

"Much of our time had been devoted to copying material from law manuals, which was comparable to trying to teach us how to run before we had been taught to walk. We discovered a method of relieving the tedium by asking the sergeant if he had ever visited a particular foreign port during his naval career, which he invariably had. Adopting what we termed his quarter-deck walk, he seemed unable to recount any experience while seated, he told us tales which were always lengthy and flattering to their author.

"Lodgings were found for us in Whitehaven. We were separated, each on a different tour of duty. For two weeks we accompanied a senior constable to learn how to work a beat and become familiar with the relative points. Very soon I became aware of a lack of the essential knowledge a constable must have to avoid mistakes. I bought some suitable books and devoted much of my spare time to mastering the basics.

"The General Strike began in May when industry and all forms of public transport stopped. Newspapers were not available, but the wireless - as it was then known - was emerging from the 'cat's whisker' receiver stage. Brief news bulletins were issued. In Whitehaven a sheet of notepaper containing the scant news was exhibited daily at the town hall. Any lorries bringing food into the town displayed a large notice stating that the vehicle and its load had been 'Passed by the Committee' - which committee we never knew! The General Strike lasted eleven days but the coal miners remained on strike until the autumn.

"When the strike began we were ordered to be careful in handling any incident. Three years earlier a strike by Whitehaven miners had erupted into a riot in which a number of police were injured. For several months nothing of any consquence occurred apart from several minor matters and domestic quarrels. When called to the latter I was always in doubt as to whether my role was that of peacemaker or umpire.

"My first real test was when patrolling in the Gins, which consisted of miners' houses. It was afternoon when I heard the sound of a disturbance. I hurried to the scene and was surprised to see two women fighting. It was something I had never witnessed before. The women were clawing each other's faces and pulling out hair. The language was foul, interspersed with uncomplimentary references as to their opponent's moral character. A small crowd appeared to be enjoying it.

"I felt like David without his sling facing Goliath. I had to do something as they had not noticed me, so I thrust myself between them, ordering them to stop, which they did. I was sure that it was only because they were so surprised that a young constable had dared to interfere. I announced that unless they went home I would arrest them. As they were both of substantial build I quickly realised to attempt to execute my threat would provide entertainment for the audience and probably prove my Waterloo. My guardian angel came to my rescue. I whipped out my pocket book to take their names and other details. To my relief they departed. Experience in later years established that women fight with the fierceness only matched when brothers fight.

"I was not involved in other matters of interest until, when on night duty in late September, the inspector came to my point at midnight and told me to accompany him. En route he explained that a young married couple were having a row in consequence of a religious difference, which was fairly frequent. A neighbour, fearing something serious might happen, had reported this at the police station.

"We turned into a narrow cul-de-sac. There were several small houses facing a high wall. It was a dark night with no street illumination because of the strike. There was a light from an uncurtained window and the sound of an angry woman's voice inside. The inspector gave a loud knock on the unlocked door and we entered. The occupants were a dark haired, attractive young woman and her young husband. Both stared at us in surprise. The room was small; kitchen and living room combined, with an old-fashioned hair-seated sofa and armchair, a small table with a burning candle stuck in a bottle in the centre, half a loaf of bread and a carving knife. The grate was empty. The inspector spoke to them in a manner born of experience, peace was restored and we left. I was instructed to visit the house before returning to the station for my refreshment at 1.00 a.m.

"When I made this visit I looked in and saw the candle was burning low in the bottle. The husband was asleep on the sofa below the window and his wife asleep in the armchair on the opposite side of the room. I was turning to leave when I saw the wife open her eyes, sit up and look across at her husband. Her lips were moving as though muttering. She rose from the chair, picked up the carving knife and began moving slowly towards her husband. Her face was contorted. I had read of evil expressions, and now I saw one. Her lips

10

were still moving; she changed her hold on the knife and held it like a dagger. She reached her sleeping husband, raised the knife and, realising she was going to stab him, I knocked hard on the window. She looked, screamed and fell to the floor in a faint.

"I hammered on the door which was locked. It was opened by the husband who was excited and declared he had not touched his wife. The knife was on the floor. I pushed it under the sofa with my foot. He had not seen it. I bent over the wife as she opened her eyes, in a whisper she said 'Why did you not let me do it?' The husband was so upset he did not hear her. I told him his wife had had a nervous attack and he must not sleep until she was fully recovered. I gave him some cigarettes. I reported to the inspector what had transpired and was told to keep a check on them. I visited them several times. The candle had burned out and all was quiet.

"Only one break-in occurred throughout the strike. The stock of a bankrupt jeweller was removed to a vacant building for public auction. A forced entry at the rear at night resulted in several items being stolen. The thief was arrested and sent to prison. However, neither a person nor house was attacked, which is remarkable when it is considered than miners were living on a mere pittance. They were helped when the butchers, grocers and other small shops allowed almost unlimited credit.

"The miners resumed work in the autumn. I gained more experience and was confirmed in making the police my career. It was interesting, revealing and unpredictable because we were dealing with people. An example of the latter was when a young colleague was on patrol at 7.00 a.m., he was approached by two agitated young women who told him their father had returned home drunk the previous night and was lying beside their dead mother. He was taken to the house and in a bedroom was the corpse. Her husband had removed the shroud from the body, was wrapped in it and had fallen asleep. He described to me during our breakfast how he had dealt with the matter. It is sufficient to state that this was in a most expeditious manner and not too gentle.

"In February 1927 I was transferred to Bampton, Westmorland, the only village near Haweswater Lake. I was lodged in a farmhouse. The reason a policeman was posted there was because a dam was to be constructed at Haweswater, also there was an outbreak of sheep scab in the district. This is a contagious disease causing loss of wool and condition. The treatment was that all sheep within a prescribed area had to be dipped twice within fourteen days in a disinfectant

11

preparation. The dippings had to be supervised by police, or Ministry of Agriculture officials.

"The day following my arrival my sergeant from Shap - which was four miles away - arrived on his motor cycle. He was a heavy, rotund man, a father figure whom I grew to like immensely. As there was no telephone I suggested adopting a method of Indian smoke-signals as a means of communication. I discovered he had a sense of humour, particularly when, on visiting Bampton, he found it necessary to call at the local hotel for the purpose of checking on the dog licence!

"I retired from the force in 1959 at Kendal as superintendent in charge of a very different force from the one I joined all these years ago."

JIM DIXON

Working with Bobbins

"I was in bobbin-making all my working life. I started off in the thirties in the old Stott Park Bobbin Mill which kept going from 1835 to 1971. The mill is a few miles from Newby Bridge. I was born five miles away from the mill. My father had worked in the old shutter works at Ulverston, now all demolished and gone. My uncle and auntie worked here in the mill.

"When it closed in 1971 they thought it would be a caravan site, but the Department of the Environment got in with some industrial archaeologists and put a restriction order on it. The Department of the Environment bought it and turned it into a museum and then English Heritage took it over. So now it will always remain like a museum. When visitors come along I take them round the mill and tell them all about the bobbin industry.

"I won't swop my accent for anybody. Some people come up after I've taken them round and say my dialect's strange to them, but I won't swop it for anybody. Accent in the Lake District varies almost from valley to valley. Go over Kendal way and it changes. Go up to Millom, it's different there. Even within a few miles there's a change..

"Last century the old bobbin masters, men like Jeremiah Coward, opened bobbins mills all over Cumberland, Westmorland and Furness. Stott Park was one of them. They supplied the great Lancashire cotton mills with their bobbins. So many bobbins were needed that even corn mills were changed to bobbin mills to meet the demand.

"The reason for bobbin mills being in the Lake District was that there was plenty of water to drive the machinery and the wood was growing on the doorstep. Like many of the old industries it was driven first by a water-wheel, a water-wheel beside the wall. At Stott Park it was thirty-two feet in diameter and lasted for about thirty years and it was a pitch-back wheel. It drove the line-shafting with all the belts in the old part of the mill.

"After that, water-turbines were installed for producing power. A steam-engine was also brought in maybe about 1880 and it was said

13

to develop twenty horse-power. Then in 1941 two electric motors were installed. You may think there would always be plenty of rainfall and water in the Lake District, but sometimes we can run short and that is why steam power was introduced in the mill.

"Up till the electricity came in, the only form of light we had in the mill were paraffin lamps. They used to be above each machine. If you got a forty watt bulb in a bobbin mill you did well for yourself. They didn't spoil you! From my experience I can tell you bobbin mills were bitter cold spots to work in. Some winter days you were literally freezing, especially when the glass had got knocked out of the windows and sacks were nailed up. They were cold draughty places.

"Now for the making of bobbins, which meant plenty of wood and we had that all over the Lake District. We made the smallest bobbins from the biggest trees and the biggest bobbins out of the smallest trees. The smallest bobbins were the bobbins used in the old cotton reels, now made from plastic. It was plastic that killed off our bobbin trade. The very small ones were those used for putting silk on.

"As the bobbin trade was gradually dying out in the early nineteen hundreds you turned round to make anything you could, pick shafts, hammer shafts etc. Wooden toys became a big thing; wooden yo-yo's, diabolos, skipping-rope handles, toy wheels, you name it. As long as it was round and turnable you could make it in a bobbin mill.

"The wood that came into the mill to make the small bobbins used for cottons and silk was from large trees like beech and sycamore. The tree that got to the right size, approximately eighteen inches in diameter, would be thirty-five to forty years of age. That was a big tree. The tree would be cut outside and then sawn off into large circular cakes to the depths of whichever length of bobbin you wanted to make. The length of your bobbin was the thickness of that big cake of wood. The cake was then held by hand in a blocking machine. Tube saws came down on the cake at about five thousand turns a minute and the idea was to cut, just like cutting pastry, as many bobbins out of the cake of wood as you could. The last bit of the cake, as you couldn't use it again, you threw it in the firewood, in a big bag. The firewood was burned at home and the mills often sold it to people for their fires.

"You never got a nice padded seat in a bobbin mill, just an up-turned hard log and a few sacks for cushions. That was what you sat on at your blocking machine. The old blocker sat down there with his swill underneath him. The swill was a big woven basket that he threw the bobbins into. As the machine punched out the bobbins he sat there with sacks round his legs to keep warm.

"Some of these chaps worked the blocking machines all their working lives, thirty or forty years. My uncle had been a blocker all his life. He used to say to me 'If you can knock a hundred gross on in ten hours, then you can call yourself a blocker.' On a cold winter's day these machines could be lethal. There were finger ends lost in the blocking machines and that was understandable. A piece of wood could kick and there was no protection at all. It was a mark of the trade as a blocker - a chap with three finger ends taken off. My uncle lost three on one of these machines. But of course that didn't always happen, although sometimes in a man's life it did. This machine still in the mill is the only machine not made in the Lake District but by a firm in Paisley. This old machine could still operate today if the Health and Safety people would allow it.

"So much for the small bobbins cut from the big trees. Now the next type of bigger bobbins came from what is kown as coppice wood. Coppice wood grew all round this area - birch, sycamore, ash, alder, hazel and rowan. Coppicing really is a method of producing a cropping of your wood. What it means is that the trees are cut down to about six inches from ground level and from that stock you might get six to eight sprouting up - six to eight from one tree. The growing time for these is sixteen to eighteen years. You get conifer trees in the Lake Distict but they weren't used in the mills - too much resin in them. They weren't native to our area.

"The long, thinner coppice trees then came into the mill. You laid them on a support outside, a peeling horse, just like a rough log with two forks sticking up. You went down the trees with a double-handed draw knife and took little strips of bark off the trees. Then the peeled trees were moved into the coppice barn and stacked right up to the roof. The wind blew through the trees and dried them out over twelve months. But if you'd laid the trees down with the bark full on, they'd start rotting. That's a job we had when we were kiddies. We used to go down of an evening to peel these trees and get a penny a score for trees twenty-odd feet in length, three ha'pence for thirty footers. So you never made a fortune peeling trees, but it kept you out of mischief at nights.

"Coppice trees were cut on the old coppice saw into shorter lengths, about a yard long. You got that length of wood in your hand, slid it onto the saw in whatever length you wanted, sawed it off and it rolled into the swills below. Every time you filled a swill you put a nick in a piece of wood called your tally stick, to show how many you had produced. After counting the number in your first swill you didn't need to count the numbers in the others. You counted the notches on your tally stick and that was your day's output.

"A sharp coppice saw doesn't cut a finger off. It's usually a blunt one that's the danger. When you were cutting you'd maybe finish up with a piece three or four inches in length. You had to make the most of it and you weren't allowed to throw it away for firewood. That was where the danger came in. You were feeding that last bit which was lethal. A blunt circular saw has a habit of rolling the piece of wood and your hand slips. So that was the old coppice saw which was the original machine in this mill.

"Typically in the old mills the blocking saws for the small bobbins and the coppice saw for the longer ones were downstairs in the mill. All the bobbin turning was done in the rooms above. In this mill the floors gave way because the machinery got too heavy and everything was moved to the newer part of the mill. The line-shaft which is in the room above is the original one that was driven by the old water-wheel. The line-shaft in our lower room can be driven by a water turbine. It's even capable of being driven by steam power today. If we could get the steam from the engine we could drive it. The old steam-engine was installed in 1880 and it's still capable of driving everything. We had it running when the B.B.C. came to televise it. There's twenty good horse-power in it when it's going. Water power costs nothing but with steam you've got to stock your boiler which in this case is a Cornish boiler, so called because it was used for pumping engines in the old tin mines in Cornwall. It was fired by the wood shaving from the mill. At night we would bank it down with sawdust to keep the fires in. So the old steam-engine kept all the line belts flapping around to drive the machines and some noise it was.

"The heat generated by the boiler also helped to dry the wood in the drying rooms The blocks of wood were laid out for drying in the rising heat. A lot of the old bobbins were at one time dyed black for putting white cotton on. We'd dip them in boiling dye outside, then we'd bring them in to take the moisture off them before polishing them upstairs.

"Just try to imagine the old steam-engine keeping those belts flapping round and round. Anything was liable to happen with these belts above your head. Quite often one would break. Now you were never allowed to stop the line-shaft up above; everybody would have to stop work and there would be too much money lost, so you had quickly to bring your belt up and stitch the torn ends together. We didn't use metal fasteners or anything like that. Then you had to put it back on that line-shaft while it was going; hold the belt with your one hand and your stick in the other and whip it on. You had to keep your thumb sticking up in the air in an upright position. If you didn't you were in trouble. You kept your eye on it all the time.

"Boring holes in the wooden blocks could be dangerous too. Women and girls worked on the boring machines and I've seen in my time girls actually scalped on this machine. I'll tell you how. The boring bits are going round at five thousand turns a minute. The skill is to get a good tight grip of the block, take it up so far as the bit and take it back to clear itself and throw it down into the swill. You've got to make sure the hole goes in the middle at the back as it goes in the middle at the front. But on a cold winter's day you've got to watch out. You can be boring and suddenly the block snatches out of your hand. If it's just at the end of the bit, it can be lethal. The block can fly off against a wall and catapult. You could be using a boring bit anything up to ten inches in length. It's deadly spinning round at five thousand. It's with women I've seen the worst accidents. I've seen women bending down to pick up a bobbin and their hair has got caught in there and they've actually been scalped. It all happened in a few seconds - a few seconds of agony. Once the blocks were bored they went to the roughing lathe which cut the wood into the approximate shape, length and diameter of the bobbin. This left the two flanges and the barrel of the bobbin a little bit larger than it needed to be. Then a finishing lathe gave it its accurate turning, the final shape of a bobbin as we know it.

"The bobbin makers would often move all round Cumbria. I don't know whether it was itchy feet or they ran up too much on the pub's slate, but they moved from one bobbin mill to another. But they were always welcomed back. There were some real characters in those days and they were skilled men. In making different sizes of bobbin they put the right tools in the machine for the particular shapes they wanted. The skill was, if you had a job and you hadn't got the tools for it, you forged and tempered your own; you ground your own and you set your own machine with the tools to shape your bobbin. There's a lot of skill goes into it.

"On one machine where an old fellow had worked for forty years, the wooden handle he used every day was shaped to the grip of his particular hand through constant use. At the end of the week's work he used to wrap a piece of sacking round his hand with linseed oil in it and that lubricated his hand for next week. It kept him from getting blisters.

"Upstairs was the work room of the old original mill from 1835 with the big sandstone grinding wheel going round in cold water. Think of it on a cold February morning with a trough half-filled with ice-cold water. The water sloshed down your neck as you held the tool to the grindstone. You could get a lovely edge on the tool but you had to tie a sack round your neck to keep dry. There was the old blacksmith's hearth nearby to put the kettle on the boil and where the old tea-cans came out. That was our canteen. Beside it the original workbench, worn down now, could tell some stories.

"All the original bobbin machines were set up on the flat, set under the windows. They put plenty of windows in because daylight costs nowt. If they got something for nothing, they did it.

"The bobbins still had to be polished. This was done in a polishing barrel. It was the action of wood sliding against wood that did the polishing. You put the bobbins in the drum; they rubbed together as the barrel turned and you put pieces of wax in the drum with the bobbins. You can understand why they called the drums rattle boxes, from the sound the bobbins made as they rubbed against each other. The barrel was just an old rum keg. It was filled about three-quarters full for if you filled it too far up the bobbins would come round and bruise themselves. If it was three-quarters full they come over in a wave action. So the bobbins were then polished and ready for dispatch.

"When the bobbins came out of the polishing drum they were emptied onto the nearby tables. Bobbins were sold by the gross - a genuine one hundred and forty-four. The golden rule when you counted bobbins was to pick up two at a time in each hand. Thirty-six times you picked up the four and you were up to a gross. You rolled them down the chute at the end of the table into the swills underneath and then they were dumped in the sacks tied with two rabbit ears on them, so that you could carry them on your shoulders. They were weighed and from there they went down the road to Lakeside Railway Station and off they went to whatever part of the country wanted them.

"As I said, when I first started in the thirties I could make up to 12/6 a week. I've got records of when they employed girls in these mills. In 1933 girls were starting at 6d an hour and a bobbin turner could get about 1/6 to 2/-. If you were on piece-work you could increase it. It's interesting looking through old records. They show we supplied stick-grenade handles to a firm in London. There's only one country in the world that as far as I knew used stick-grenades and that was Germany. During the war we made duffle-coat toggles, tent pole tops, hammer shafts, anything that needed wood turning. But the bobbin trade is now gone, killed by plastics. The only real relic of it left in the country is the museum at Stott Park which gives you the best idea of how this old Cumbrian industry lived and died.

"The only thing that seems to be coming back now is the wooden toy. But that's got to be done commercially and it couldn't be done at Stott Park. For although the old mill has been passed by the Health and Safety people for public viewing, it could not be run commercially. So a museum it will always be, where people from all over can come and see what was done in this part of Cumbria."

HILDA FOSTER

Farmer's Wife

"I was born in a little cottage up in Cartmel in 1922. I went to school at Staveley in Cartmel. It was my granny who did all the milking by hand on our small farm. They worked hard in those days. My granny and grandpa actually built a café by the road. My granny did all the labouring, up the scaffolding and the lot. Who on earth would do that today? I used to help them.

"I walked two miles in clogs from the little farm to the school. I had a very good teacher. If it was a very cold day, she used to make us a cup of cocoa. She really looked after us. You seldom get that kind of caring today. In those days we used slates in the infants and we had slate pencils. Slate pencils were a Christmas present for me. When I got a handbag with a shilling in it I thought I'd got a really marvellous present. What a difference today, yet we were satisfied and happy.

"At eleven we went to Leven Valley Central School. We had a cookery teacher there that started me off in cooking. My grandson goes to that school now. I really enjoyed school. We'd climb trees in the playtime. It was great fun.

"Ever since I was fourteen I've made my own living. When I left I was three weeks finding a job. I got a place at Witherslack, living-in and looking after a family. I did all the baking on an oil stove and I could bake on that oil-stove, you'd never believe it! I had watched my granny a lot and she taught me many things. From the beginning I had to, what we say in these parts, 'shape myself'. I began with 10 shillings a week and finished up with £1.

"I worked there till I was married and I was married very young. I had a wonderful husband. He was good. It was one day, I was on my bicycle going home and I met him coming up and I wondered who he was. We both turned round and we both nearly fell off our bikes. We got to know each other after that. He used to push both our bikes up that terrible hill, the How Top. I only had Sunday afternoons off and he'd come for me. He joined the Coldstream Guards and we got married then. Before coming north again we lived in London and Somerset. Farmers were badly needed then and Jim was chosen

20

along with other Guardsmen to go on this farm. The farmer asked his officer if he could have Jim for six months. Now the officer lived close to the farm and to get Jim, the farmer had to give him butter and flitches of bacon and so on, black-marketing my husband to keep him. He was in plain clothes but got into his Guards uniform once a week just to go for his army pay. That would be around 1943.

"Just after the war we went into our first farm at Witherslack, a forty-seven acre farm which we got rent free and little wonder, for it was a total mess. It had been used for timber and what was left we just ploughed into the land. I remember we arrived one dinner-time and the man who was there hadn't got out. He had a job getting the bed out. He got my husband to help him. I had to laugh as he had got it fastened up in his braces. The man had to load up a wood wagon before we could get in. Asphalt covered the floor and I had to get down and scrape that floor before it was re-flagged.

"I thought I'd take in visitors to make a bit more money as I had three children. The house had five bedrooms but no bathroom. I took in two Polish men who had waited on after the war and who became helpers on the farm. I remember one incident when I had had them only a week. I was making sausages and mash. I had a great big round frying pan. The sausages were ready and I had a boiler at the side full of hot water, ready for my husband to feed the calves. At the time he was over at his father's who was ill. Anyway the sausages fell into the water meant for the calves. I got my toasting fork and got them all out and put them back in the frying pan with a bit of fresh fat and they never knew till this day. I had to get a ladling can and empty the boiler because I couldn't give the calves greasy water and then I had to pump it and fill it again. You see there was no water to drink in the house and I had to carry drinking water across a field and pump it in the house. I had to burn my kindling sticks to get the water hot again before the men came back. When they sat down to eat those sausages I couldn't have had my meal with them or I would have burst out laughing.

"I made all my custard pies and jams. Killing a pig was quite a do in those days. You put it on a long sort of table with slats. The pig was put on this and its throat was cut. There was I with a bucket and a stick, catching the blood and stirring it so that it wouldn't clot, I put it near the fire and kept stirring it. That was for my black puddings. You had to do all sorts of jobs on the farm. My black pudding made with barley, fat, sage and different herbs were lovely. I got the skins from the pigs' intestines. You wasted nothing.

"If you had seen my kitchen in those days! When it had been cleaned out it was lovely, scrubbed white top of the dresser, no polishing in those days - black-lead grate and emery-paper shine on the fender. It was great when I got an alladin lamp. It was never later than six when I got up in the morning.

"I'll never forget the day the horse came into the house. It got up the few steps. I had just scrubbed my big room out which had a flag floor and an old-fashioned black-leaded grate. I had done a bake, for you had a baking day, and I put it on a dresser which was about an inch thick wood - all my gingerbread. I'll never forget it. I had my bucket of water in the back kitchen. I had washed backwards in the back kitchen. This great horse came up the steps, right into the kitchen I had just cleaned. It went all round, knocking off my baking. I had an awful job to turn it. What a mess it made! As it went out it stood on my bucket of water and squashed my bucket and broke a gingerbread dish I had made my food in. What a job I had to get the horse out of the house.

"My husband came in later. I said 'The horse has been in the house.' He said 'Don't be funny.' I showed him the bucket, 'I couldn't have squashed the bucket, could I?' I don't think he believed me. He sat down for tea with the two Polish men who helped him on the farm. Suddenly the horse appeared again and up the steps it came. He had quite a job to back it out. While this was going on our little dog kept yapping and pulling at the hairs on the horse's legs and the horse suddenly lifted the pail and plopped it right on the dog's head. We never saw the puppy for two days. It had its funny side too.

"We just had four or five milk cows on the farm. We bought them for about thirty-five pounds each. We had a small field of two and a half acres; we got ten carts of dockens from it, docken roots - ten carts off two and a half acres! It shows you the mess it was in to start with. As the whole acreage was only about forty acres, my husband used to go out and do the dykes for other people in the area. He'd also pick damsons. But I loaded every cart of hay in the haymaking for years. I remember going down a steep field with the horse and cart. We were loaded and I fell off. I was covered with hay. One of the Polish men was helping to load. He pushed the fork up and shouted 'Where the hell are you?' I couldn't help laughing: I was underneath the hay. I got up and carried on. You never stopped in those days.

"I had never fastened a cow till I got married. The first time my husband came and said 'Will you tie these cows up?' I did it from that day onwards. We sold the milk to the Milk Marketing Board for 1/

22

11 the gallon. They collected the twelve gallon milk churns which we left at the road end. We had a motor-bike with a box on it and we used to take them down on that to the road end.

"One day my husband asked me to feed the cows. I had to climb the ladder and throw the hay down on top of a hole but it wouldn't go through. When I came down I tried with my fork to push it through, but it wouldn't go through to the gangway in front of the cows. I knelt down and when pushing it through I went through with it. I fell eight feet and broke an arm. But then you didn't go to the doctor in those days, did you? You bound it and kept it till it got better. The cows jumped back. You never heard such a clatter. I daren't go near that hole for ages, I had such a funny feeling.

"I had then three children and one was only four months old when we went to the farm. One of my boys, the youngest, is now a policeman. Then there's Alan who farms at Sow How in Cartmel and was Shepherd of the Year and won national and international sheep-dog competitions. He is wonderful with dogs. Another is a private collector for biology firms. He gets spiders, centipedes, frogs, toads. He has a special permit for alcohol. For instance he had an order from America for seventeen thousand starfish. He had a friend who went out on a boat from Morecambe. They knew the tides. They'd pick up the starfish and rush them back. This friend was a builder. He had a great big pool where he was building a house. They had to get them into this water. Then when they died we had to work like mad - for I helped - to get them into the alcohol to preserve them. Then they were sent to America. He also collects different types of worms. He sends them to private collectors and firms who distribute them to colleges for study in biology and that kind of thing. Frederick, another boy, is a greengrocer with two shops and a market stand. Altogether I've had five children, including a fine daughter.

"We moved into a bigger farm in the Witherslack area, 78 acres. We still had outside toilets and no electric at first. This was also a milking farm and we had damsons. We had that many damsons, Jim and I one year picked eight score short of three tons. Two of our boys picked the bottom, they were quite small then. We got 12/6 a score for the damsons. That was great. That went for more cows. We were building up all the time, selling off cattle and putting the money in the bank.

"We lived as much as possible off the land. I used to make lots of rabbit pies. When we moved to our second farm my husband said 'First these rabbits will have to go. Twenty rabbits eat as much as one sheep.' Off they went, my husband and the Pole, and provided me with rabbits and I got 5/- for a big one and a little one; that kept me going all summer. I had to do all the gutting. I'd sell them to a butcher and that kept me in housekeeping money. Also there were so many daffodils the children used to go and pick them. We got 6d a bunch for the first lot. I bunched them in a shed when they had gone to bed. From 6d a bunch they came down to 3d a bunch. We collected £12 which we put in a glass jar and that bought their sandals. That's how we lived.

"Then my husband found a third farm up at Satterthwaite and that was one hundred and seventy acres. We had sheep at this farm which did better than the cows. One of the Polish men stayed with us. He was a very good worker. Until John was bigger I had still a lot of farm jobs to do at Satterthwaite, including loading the hay. In the first week of haytime my husband took seriously ill and nearly died. I was a month off having my last child. John and Frederick helped out. Alan was a marvellous farmer. When Jim was in hospital, Alan milked. Alan was the only one interested in farming as a career and he has certainly been a success in it. From the very beginning he showed an interest in farming, haymaking, milking and so on. I had to keep him off school such a lot when Dad was ill. We'd never let Alan lift up the milk - the old stockman used to lift up the milk to let it run into the cooling system - but he could milk and he knew exactly what he was doing. He was farming mad in those days. He used to get up at six o'clock before he was eleven. He'd go round the sheep and when Jim was going out Alan was coming back. So when Jim was ill I had to keep him off school as much as necessary. He has turned out well, has Alan.

"My husband was so ill we had to sell up and we came to live in Grange-over-Sands. He was a very conscientious man and he had a sense he was letting us down by having to leave the farm. I took in visitors and my husband went down to get a job. He was a coalman at first, then went on to work with Glaxo . I had loads of friends and was full up with visitors. We had lovely people and I did dinner, bed and breakfast. I had plenty to do when the visitors were around in summer, but when it came to winter I though 'Goodness gracious, what am I to do?' I've always been so active and busy. I've always been interested in the elderly, I had a talk with my doctor and through him got an old lady of ninety to look after. I couldn't turn her out when it came to spring and my usual visitors began to arrive. So I thought, instead of having visitors, why not look after three old people all the time? I had a Methodist minister and his wife come for a month. They were so happy they said could they come and stay always with me? He had had a stroke and couldn't walk properly and she was blind. I told them to think carefully before giving up their home as they had only been here a month. But they insisted and in the end I had three permanent old people to look after. When the last one died I thought I'd give over but my husband's mother came for about four years, for she couldn't do anything for herself. I turned a downstairs room into a bathroom. After that I thought this is the end. But would you believe it, an old lady came just for a fortnight but persuaded me to let her stay and she was eighteen months with me. I think these old folk felt secure and happy, and I must admit I always have been a glutton for work.

"My hushand died at 64 and I was absolutely lost. I just had to do something. A chance meeting with a lady on the train to Morecambe led to me getting in touch with an agency for old folk. Through it I went as a companion to an 85 year old in Hampstead in London. I must say the family was astounded. Did their mother know what she was doing? My stay in London with that amazing old Jewish lady is a story in itself. I found out that nobody before me had stayed more than a week, she was so difficult. But with all my experience of life and of the elderly I was able to handle her and we finished up with a good relationship. Looking back on it, it was quite a carry-on. She called me at nine in the morning and I had three different kinds of oil to rub her. When she took her clothes off at night I had to shake everything out of the window and we were three storeys up. I used to think 'Gosh, if anything drops here' Then every garment was put on a clothes-hanger and they had to be put in another room, not in the same room with her. It was quite a carry-on. There were just her, me and cook who came at ten and left at half-past three. Despite her rudeness at times I won her over and she wanted me to go to Germany for a month with her. She used to sing and I knew she was happy with me. After that I went to Whitchurch and looked after a lovely old lady there, but she died.

"As a farmer's wife and farmer's mother I was particularly pleased when my son Alan won national competitions at trials. Alan's great interest in dogs developed through his wife's father who was a farm manager and trained dogs. Alan was on television with his dog representing England. I've got the video of it. We always had dogs on the farm. Our dog was the only thing on the farm my husband wouldn't sell. I said to Alan when we were talking about how he trained them 'Do you ever get mad with them? Do you ever hit them?' He said 'No. If they make a mess of things, they know by the tone of voice. They know when something's wrong.' It's really marvellous to watch how he handles them. It's interesting watching him train two together, the one lying quietly while the other is working. They react to his mood all the time. Once when he didn't win a competition he said it was his own fault. It was his nervousness and it affected the dogs.

"Looking back at the family's childhood they were great days too. All the boys were in the Boys' Association for running. They were sport mad. I used to put my head out of the bedroom window of an evening. Alan, Frederick, John and Dad were all lined-up in the field. I used to shout at the top of my voice 'Ready, steady, go!' and off they went. That is a happy memory.

"I was almost forty when I was persuaded to run in the Russland Sports. The boys ran too. It was a wet day and I had Jim's wellingtons on and a pleated skirt and I had his stockings underneath my wellingtons. So I said 'If I run I'll run in Jim's stockings,' so I took the wellingtons off and I ran and I won. I was really fit at that time. I thought that was it over, but they told me there were other heats. I ran again and I actually won and got 15/-. That was some day, despite the rain.

"I've had a great family. That and a sense of humour have kept me going through a life of hard work."

EDDIE HARRISON

Working with Slate

"Slate quarrying in Cumbria was very often a family occupation. My grandfather, my father, my uncle, my nephew all worked in it. My grandfather retired just before I started. There must have been six or seven Coopers at Burlington Quarry, all relations. There were Cowards, five or six Steels. There were six Simpsons.

"Burlington Quarries are about half-way between Greenodd and Ulverston, up on Gawthwaite Moor or Kirkby Moor. It's the biggest quarry in England, about nine miles from Barrow, and its been on the go for over two hundred years. At first it produced just roofing slate but nowadays it produces architectural slate like window sills, facing slabs and so on. Also it turns out riven slate for flooring tiles.

"There are slate quarries in different parts of Cumbria producing different colours of slate. Ours at Kirkby is blue-grey. The others are different shades of green: olive at Honister, light-green at Kirkstone, olive green at Broughton Moor, light green at Elterwater and so on.

"I was born in the small hamlet of Beanthwaite right against the quarries. You could throw a stone from the quarries right down to Beanthwaite. That was in 1919. I went to school at Grizebeck, just a mile down the road. I left when I was 14 and started work at the quarry in 1933, when I got 10/- a week.

"My father had to speak for me to get into the quarry and I was only too thankful to get a job as times then weren't easy. As a boy you just did the small jobs the older men gave you. They didn't give you much because every skilled man was on piece-work and they worked in small groups or 'companies'. So you worked pretty well on your own and you were taught by a senior apprentice. Now and then a senior man would say to you 'Come and do this or that,' and after that you'd go off and do your own little jobs. You'd do this for two years and then somebody would speak for you to get you into one of the groups or 'companies' as they were called. Once in you were taught and it was the men who paid you, paid you for what you produced. So the men made sure you worked. There was no room for passengers.

27

"At the quarry there must have been fourteen little companies. Each company would put their mark on their own rock which would be worked by its own little gang of men. You'd have a price for each ton of slate, different prices for different qualities. We were paid monthly for whatever we produced less costs, like paying men up on the tips for tipping the slate or paying for the use of horses. You paid for your own gunpowder, for the blacksmith's drills, hammers, tools. After these costs were taken off, what was left was divided up into the number of days, and it might come out, as when I started, at 9/9d a day for skilled men. I gave my wages to my mother. Times were hard then.

"I got 10/- a week. My father got 30/- a week. Now when I was a boy I did a lot of fell running and I could get as much on a Saturday, if I won, as my father could get for a week's work. I could win £1 or £1-5s.-0d. or £1-10s.-0d. if it was something special.

"You were never finished learning about the different jobs in producing the slates. Great slabs of rocks were won from the quarry by blasting with gunpowder. In my time a bogey could carry a piece of rock one and a half to two tons in weight. Nowadays the big wagons can carry up to ten tons.

"Slabs of rock were got ready for splitting or 'riving' the slate. Skill not brute strength is needed for this. In my day a skilled river split the slabs with hammer and chisel for the required thickness. A dresser would then shape the slate into a tile. Nowadays with machinery a river can produce up to two tons of roofing slate a day.

"Good craftsmen in those days were very much appreciated. Everybody wanted to be a good craftsman and wanted a good craftsman in the little gang - to make money. Today that feeling doesn't apply, for with modern machinery everything is sawn for them. Where you had really bad rock and you were working all day, cutting and splitting, and trying to save as much as possible out of your rock, you had to look after what rock you had. That's why you had to be a good craftsman.

"I said our Burlington slate was blue-grey. It was the easiest to work. You can cut it both ways and it splits the finest. The green rock is harder and coarser. It's not so easy to work and it won't cut as thin. But it's still a very, very good quality slate. At Burlington two and a quarter inches is the width of a wedge. Now there are eight slates in that, so you middle it, then middle it and middle it. That gives you your eight slates. But with green you've got to take more because you can't split it so fine, and it's a lot slower process. The green is dearer.

Say for instance a man at Burlington was splitting a ton a day, in green he might do only fifteen hundred weight. It's slower to handle it and work. If they are both getting the same wage, the green has got to be dearer because you can't produce as much in a day.

"Burlington slate has gone all over the world and some of the finest buildings in this country are covered in Burlington slate. You find it on many of the bigger houses in London; Harry Lauder's house in Scotland was covered with it. I think Inveraray Castle also used it and other ancient places in Scotland. In my day houses all used roofing slate. After the war, as I said, the use of slate was extended for architectural uses and people used it for many purposes. The slate products in gift shops are of course just one little side-line. These are made by individuals who come along and buy the slate and make these products. But on a big scale the slates are exported all over the world - at costs of over a million pounds a job. So slate is really big business. Nowadays with all the modern machinery they are using rock they couldn't have used in the old days. So I think the industry which has been going for over two hundred years still has a good future. The machinery can make more economical use of the resources of the quarry.

"In my young days the work and conditions were very hard. We worked in a little shed with a wooden door you could lift on. You had your bottle of cold tea and little tin of sandwiches. At times when conditions were very bad your tea would be frozen when you came to drink it. There were no facilities then, no canteens. They were tough men and there really wasn't a lot of illness, just a few accidents. They were hard men but there was a great feeling of comradeship. Everybody knew everybody and if there *was* an illness people rallied round. When there was a death there used to be a man come round doing what they called 'bidding'. He'd tell families what time the funeral was and where it would take place.

"Beanthwaite was only a small village, four cottages and a farm. There was an inn there, the Buckhorn Inn, now closed. My grandfather, William Rawlinsen, was the last landlord there. I was born in the inn but later we moved up the road about two hundred yards to the cottage. Now, Buckhorn Inn was close to the quarry and my grandfather told me that in the very old days when the men got their pay, their first stop was the Buckhorn. But their wives used to be waiting for them there and made sure they got their money before the men went in and went on the spree. They came from the area all round Beanthwaite, Grizebeck, Kirkby and Gawthwaite. Later they came from further afield as transport was laid on from Millom, Ulverston and right round the area.

"My wife and I went to Grizebeck School together. She was a Heaton. Her brother worked in slate. While I was away during the war she lived in Millom. Then we settled down in Kirkby. We went back to Millom then, when I retired, we came to live here in Barrow. We had two boys, one now an accountant and the other works in the Crown Court in Preston.

"Looking back I remember some real characters, great old slate-workers. Bert Fryer was one. He was a keen sportsman in his younger days. He was a football referee and cricket umpire. He trained me as a fell runner. Everybody knew Bert. He had a sense of humour and was in both good things and in devilment. He was into everything - a character on his own. Jim Gaskell was another. He used to go on the spree when he had money in his pocket. I've known him to have a fortnight off. He was a rock man, that is he worked at the quarry face, blasting out the rock with dynamite. He was a good hand at 'winning' the rock, as we call it. He used to smoke a clay pipe. Everything had been cleaned up and they were ready for a shot. Now Jim didn't rush up and say 'We'll do this.' He'd walk about nearly for a day thinking of all that needed attention. But once he had made up his mind, he gave each one his orders and his particular job. He was a good man. Once a blast blew back in his face. He always had a blue speckly face. This would happen in a big shot at the quarry.

"When I started I worked in a small shed. In those days you were in and out all the time. You had to bring your rock in and wheel your slate out. You pushed a wagon with your waste to the tip. The essential thing was, in the cutting and dressing, you should have as little waste as possible.

"In the olden days at blasting time they used to put up a red flag and sound a horn at the hut above the quarry face which was about four hundred feet. They'd warn the people ten minutes before the hour, and five minutes before the hour and on the hour. After five minutes past the all-clear sounded. Usually they had an old man in the horn house. Down in the quarry you could look up and see the red flag up above you warning you that blasting would take place; then you'd hear the horn go. One day the old man in the horn house was off sick, so they put up a young man, an apprentice called Harry This-tlethwaite. Some of the men working underneath shouted to him 'What time is it, Harry?' One chap yelled 'It bloody well can't be.' Harry shouted 'Look for yourself' and threw the clock down to him!

Needless to say that stopped the clock.

"When I started there would be about twelve horses that pulled the wagons up and down. They had lads driving these horses. They weren't actually serving their time. They were more like labourers. One lad said to another 'My horse is stronger than yours.' They all had their names, Boxer, Mabel, Dolly, Jack and so on. So they put their two horses back to back and put a chain on and pulled to see which one was stronger, a kind of tug of war. Old Mr Jones, who was the boss then, soon put a stop to that lot.

"The industry is quite important for Cumbria. Burlington employs about one hundred and seventy. Mr Fecitt has his workshop at Skelurth Bridge. His quarry is up at Kirkston Pass. Burlington is the biggest in Cumbria, it is a very progressive firm with young forward-looking directors. Mr Cavendish of Holker Hall is the owner of Burlington. The firm is full of new ideas for the future.

"I've been one of the lucky ones in my job. Some men went into the industry and did the same job all their lives. I did the different jobs and became a foreman. I had a trip to Germany for the firm; this was under the Williams and Glyn's Export United Travel Award Scheme. The scheme was devised to encourage British firms to send shop-floor personnel abroad. I was among the 1979 award winners and after several interviews won the award for the North-West. We exported slate to Germany and I suppose I was promoting that. I stayed with our agent out there and toured around with him, interviewing architects, slaters and builders. Then Mr Ogden one of our directors asked me if I'd undertake sales of slate in Cumbria. I did that and thoroughly enjoyed it and only wish I could have started that twenty year earlier. I don't think I would have been satisfied limiting it to Cumbria.

"Mine has been an interesting and satisfying life in one of Cumbria's oldest industries."

MURRAY HODGES

A Cumbrian Parson

"About 1905 my father got the living at Kirklinton, about nine miles from Carlisle. I'm eighty-five so I think I can have my nationalisation papers as a member of the county. We did our shopping every fortnight with a horse and cart into Carlisle. My father was a good driver and picked a good horse and we did the nine miles in an hour. I remember, though it has disappeared now, the old Emperor café. I had a mild passion for sardines on toast which was satisfied there.

"When I was very young my health had not been too good and my education had been somewhat restricted. I went on to Limehouse School near Wetheral, a long-bow shot from Rose Castle. In 1911 my father was offered the living of Christchurch in Cockermouth, now a town of about six thousand people with one parson looking after the lot. There used to be two vicars and two clerics. Wordsworth's family home wasn't all that far from the church. I've been over it a few times. I'm not sure if the Wordsworths were connected with the church but I should imagine they were.

"In 1917 I passed the entrance to Rossall, a public school on the Lancashire coast between Blackpool and Fleetwood. I had played soccer at Limehouse. I used to play outside right and then inside right. When I got to Rossall I played rugby at which I was completely useless but since then, seeing people who really could play it, on the television and in the playing field, I've realised it's a much more intelligent game than I thought when at school.

"At Rossall I studied classics and then I passed what was the school certificate and higher certificate. In those days we had to specialise; I had one year at the higher certificate in classics and moved into group two in history and French. In sport I managed to get my house-colours for running and gymnastics, although I suspect I had no great speed unless I was scared of being late for class or chapel!

"I went on to Kings in Cambridge but please don't ask me to sing. Increasingly I love music but I'm not tone perfect! How did I become a minister? Well, my father was a minister and a very good one. He

Alan, Hilda Dixon's son, a national sheep-dog trials champion. *(Chapter 3. Farmer's wife)*

Above:
Tom Barbour joined the Cumbrian constabulary in 1926 and finished as Superintendent-in-charge, Kendal.
(Chapter 1. Bobby on the beat)

Left:
Eddie Harrison, boring holes in slates.
(Chapter 4. Working with slate)

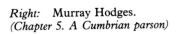

Right: Murray Hodges.
(Chapter 5. A Cumbrian parson)

Below: The church at Mungrisdale.

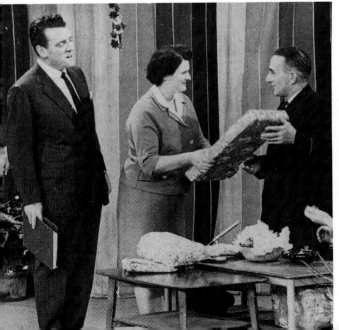

Left:
Mary Nolan.
(Chapter 6. Postmistress at Boot)

In 1960 Mary went to London to present a gift to local postman Dick Bancroft, on the Eamonn Andrews Show.

Below:
Ralph Cannon.
(Chapter 7. Reservoir Keeper)

Left;
Ralph made an inspection of Fisher Tarn every morning, for leaks and necessary repairs.

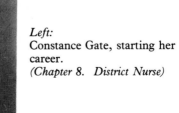

Left:
Constance Gate, starting her career.
(Chapter 8. District Nurse)

Right:
Bob Clarke.
(Chapter 9. Farmer, wrestler and horn-stick maker)

Above:
Cumberland wrestling style.

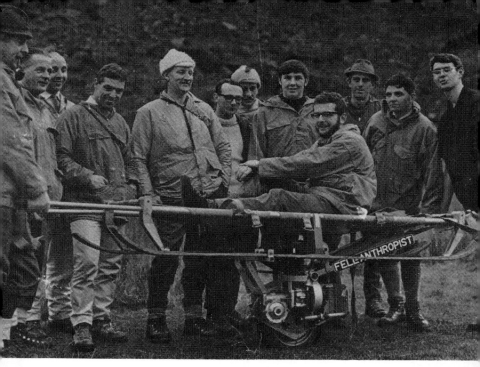

Above: Brian Stilling, second on left, with a mobile mountain rescue stretcher invented locally. *(Chapter 10. Mountain Search and Rescue)*

Right: Blanche Bott. *(Chapter 11. Schoolteacher)*

Below: The Old School.

Edna Hall.
*(Chapter 12. Mayor and
Pet Shop Owner)*

Right:
Mayor Edna with Prince
Charles (1976).

Above: Mr and Mrs Bob Cleasby at Buckingham Palace
Garden Party - Bob a representative of British Legion.
(Chapter 13 Pt.1. Making Shoes)

Left:
Sherpas Tensing and
Chanjup examining
the Everest Boots
made by a 'K'
craftsman.

Right:
Jim Major.
*(Chapter 13 Pt.2.
Making Shoes)*

THE EYELET
THE **K** SHOE MAGAZINE

OCTOBER 1949   THREEPENCE

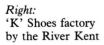

JIM MAJOR

Left:
Jim Major on the
cover of the First
Edition of the
company magazine,
1949.

Right:
'K' Shoes factory
by the River Kent

and my mother were remembered by many of their congregations. One person showed me a photograph taken in 1907 of a football team and my father was in it holding the little black bag. I had been thinking of going into teaching - I think in the way many people do, often the wrong people, when they're wondering what to do with their children. In fact later as a minister I used to teach in my church schools and I loved that: I talked to an old man who said 'I suppose you've never thought of being ordained for the ministry.' It was then I had a kind of feeling God was calling me. Something inside seemed to be arguing. My father was delighted.

"I went to Ridley Hall and took the ordination examination. I returned in 1935 to the Diocese of Carlisle and Bishop Williams was willing to ordain me. He was a remarkable man with a Gordon Harker face and so was often known as 'the burglar.' He was in the diocese up to 1948. I remember at my ordination retreat he told us, among other things, rather a charming story. One day he saw this man wandering round Rose Castle and helped him to find the door - Rose Castle that a later bishop called 'my tied cottage' - he was a farmer that Bishop Williams was going to visit in the next day or two. He wanted to tell the bishop what was wrong with the parish. This being the early twenties he considered the Church was doing nothing for the ex-servicemen of the parish. He said 'The Church has done nowt for the ex-service chaps. Now the Wesleyans, they got up a fund for us. But what have they done with it? They've gone and bought a piano with it. They opened piano last week an'all. Half-way through t'evening, there was blood and teacups flying, and that's how they opened piano.'

"I well remember when Bishop Williams retired in 1948, we had given him a portrait which was done in triplicate - one for hanging up in Rose where it is now, one that he could take away and the third went to the Academy. I remember him saying 'This one is what I hope I am, this one is what the artist conceives me to be and this is what the diocese feared that I was.' He had a good sense of humour.

"The bishop allowed me a year with my father in Cockermouth as his curate there. After that I had to look for a job. I found there was a curacy at the Rossall Mission in Manchester. The parish was on the Oldham side of Manchester. They were a friendly people. It was there I became involved again with the scouts. I hadn't been involved with them since my schooldays. It was in Manchester, too, I got into my plimsolls and shorts and did a bit of jogging. In those days in Manchester you weren't supposed to jog in public but in the recreation ground, I played tennis there and got to know people, but going for a jog up the main Oldham road was just a thing people never thought of doing. I noticed one or two men on their way to work looking curiously at me. There was one policeman on point duty who shouted at me 'Hey, th'ar a' reet for Wigan!' That apparently was not a compliment.

"I might have stayed there longer but I got word my father back in Cockermouth was seriously ill and possibly dying. The war had been a big strain on him - he had gone off to it in his early fifties. He was mentioned twice in Field-marshall Douglas Haig's dispatches. Father was a garrison chaplain in Belgium. He wrote home once to say that when he returned on duty, his office had vanished while he was away! He had a sense of humour which was illustrated by one of his young men who was his church warden. Four of them had been having a foursome at golf near Cockermouth, the hole was a one shot hole and somebody behind them had hit a shot without waiting to see if the green was clear. The ball landed plump among the four of them. The young men were annoyed and said to father 'Chuck it in the hedge, padre. Kick it down the hill,' that kind of thing. But Father said 'No, I have a better idea' he quietly picked up the ball and put it in the hole. It meant when the chap got back to the club-house he'd have to stand his pals a bottle of whisky. He thought that was the best way of punishing him! That was typical of my father. Fortunately he made a remarkable recovery, but soon after that, on doctor's advice, he retired.

"Then I went as a curate for four years at the big parish church in Kendal, from 1927 to 1931. It had five aisles and a wonderful organ. On the north aisle you see hanging a helmet and sword. There was a dashing fellow called Bellingham who lived on an island in Windermere, probably at the time of the Civil War. He came into the church during a service on horseback with his sword drawn. Now in those days lots of people carried swords, which apparently gave some status. Immediately there was a rustling of steel all round the congregation. Blades began to flash and he saw he was in real trouble. He whirled round, dug his spurs in and made off, but his helmet came off and he lost his sword.

"When I was at Kendal I found some of the young men were keen on athletics and I got quite involved in sport. I bowled and played tennis. I got involved especially in the young men's club and helped them with their table tennis of which I knew a bit as I had played it for a long time. I did a bit of running with them. We had a running competition with one of the local Free Churches, the Zionists. We thought it would be a good idea to have a run against the local grammar-school, but I found out something interesting - they were very shy of professionals in running and several of my boys who ran with me were pro's. The headmaster refused me outright. He said 'You've got professionals running with you.' I said 'But they wouldn't be running for money.' He maintained that the fact they were professionals would professionalize all his boys because they'd run against them. It was a pity, but there it was.

"One of the problems of a country parson in the Lake District, particulary in lonely and less accessible places, is that of transport, for yourself and for other less mobile people. Fortunately I was always keen on driving, either bikes, motor-bikes or cars. In Cockermouth in the early days I had a 250 B.S.A.. That was in 1926. Then in Kendal I got an Austin 7. As well as being useful in pastoral work it was useful in getting home to Embleton near Cockermouth when I had a day off. They were, I suppose, good little cars and you even see some on the roads today, but in Kendal everything seemed to go wrong with mine. It was the only new car I ever bought in my life and it cost a whole £140. Twice the dynamo went wrong, the battery went wrong, all the electrics went wrong. At last I changed to a 500 c.c. touring Rudge motor-cycle. It was quite exciting as it had the sort of acceleration that could tug at your armpits. I'm lucky because, including motor-cars and motor-bikes, I toured on the roads of Cumbria for fifty years without an accident.

"The curate who was senior to me in Kendal was an unusual chap. He had a natural gift for dramatics. In those days he would get £300 for the church by putting on a musical show. He would use his holiday going to London and seeing musical shows there and getting tips for his own shows. One occasion I remember because it involved the use of weapons. A professional had said you must always be careful with the use of weapons in a dramatic show. In this case the story involved a transgressor in some biblical situation running for his life with avengers after him. Everyone was in costume. My senior curate, who had been in the First War in the East and had got friendly with some Arabs, had a splendid Arab attire and he was sitting as a great sheikh. The man was running with the avengers after him. I remember being dressed in costume and running up the passage in the main hall between the rows in the audience. I thought 'With this large scimitar I'm carrying, if one of us slips I could damage the man in front of me.' Then I glanced over my shoulder and saw a large man bounding behind me with a spear nearly in my spine. In the end all was well. It was an interesting bit of bible study, dramatically done!

"When I was at Kendal a young minister had got the living at Kentmere about twenty minutes drive from Kendal. He was taking a service at the next parish at Longsleddale. His parish clerk there always gave out the notices, so he gave him the list of notices to read then he suddenly remembered something he had left out. The Vicar of Longsleddale was ill and the young man had promised to give up his own evensong and take the vicar's evening service for him. He leaned over to his parish clerk and said 'There's one extra notice I forgot to list. There will be no evening service next Sunday night as I shall be officiating at Longsleddale.' The parish clerk didn't forget and he announced 'There 's just yin notice. There'll be nae service next Sunday neet as't vicar's off fishing at Langsleddale!'

"Suddenly out of the blue I found myself offered the country living at Mungrisdale behind Skiddaw, twelve miles from Penrith and ten miles from Keswick. The name is interesting. The dale, of course, is the dale. 'Gris' is where they kept the pigs. The 'Mun' part comes from St. Mungo or Kentigern who was the patron saint of the church. It was a country parish of three or four hundred, entirely farming. I visited all the farms and this is where a car was useful. By now I had stopped being a motor-cyclist and I had got a Morris two-seater, I think a 1927 model. I was getting £7 a week and couldn't afford to get it re-bored. I've never had a car that used so much oil.

"One experience I remember with that Morris. I had been visiting and started up the car. I had been moving half a mile an hour from rest, all of a sudden the steering wheel just went round in my hand. I went underneath the car and found the drag link and steering link were just hanging apart. I pushed them together and didn't seem to get much tightening on the screw. I drove very slowly to the nearest garage at Keswick. I had done about a dozen miles at a crawl. The man took one look at it and said 'Man, how did you get here? Half the balljoint's missing!' Country parsons had their transport problems in those days.

"Mungrisdale was a lovely little church with a three-decker pulpit. It was there I began to preach extempore. I had tried it once before at Kendal but it didn't work. After coming out of a church like Kendal, to see a large oil lamp in front of my three-decker pulpit! I didn't realise that ring burner was shooting out sixty candle-power, but when it came to the state prayers at the end of the service I found I couldn't read it. I took up my sermon notes and they might have been written in Chinese. So I had to have a go without them. So for years after that I just said the sermon to myself till I knew it. That way it shrank and shrank and I was happy with it.

"I was happy in this country parish. In areas like this you meet real characters. There was one up at Blakebeck Farm. The Mandales were what you call 'old standards.' They had been farming round there, from Greystoke half-way back to Keswick, for generations. There was Hutch Mandale and Joe, his father, whom I didn't know. He was before my day and was an even greater character than his son. In the father's day the water supply was at last coming through from Penrith. The foreman set his men digging across Joe's land without so much as a by your leave. The old man came up in a rage and the foreman lost his temper too. He said 'I don't care what you say, old fellow. I've got my certificate here from the Council. That's good enough for me.' Then Joe got out his big pocket-watch and said quiety, 'All I can say is, if you're not off my land in ten minutes, summat'll happen.' In ten minutes to the tick a rather nasty bull came out. The men took quick avoiding action, dropping their picks as they ran. Joe was standing there chuckling with his watch in his hand, he shouted to the foreman 'Show him your certificate, man, and it'll be a' reet.' That was the end of the argument.

"There was an old lady at Mungrisdale, a real character. She had an old grandfather clock that she reckoned was always right. It was two and a half hours walk to the nearest railway station. She didn't trust herself to buses. It was a good two miles, anyway, to the bus stop and at least another mile to the railway station. She always used to set off to catch the eleven o'clock at quarter to eight. She never altered her grandfather clock which she declared was always right. I actually once took her out in a motor-car. That was a record. She was the schoolmistress, a very good one. On one occasion she had been taking the story of our Lord with her class. She was talking about the rich man, Dives, and the poor man Lazarus lying at his gate. Just to show the children what a selfish pig Dives had been she had done a lot of homework, a complete list of what a rich man of that time would have had on his table. She turned to the children and asked 'Now children, how would Dives feel?' A boy's hand, Joe Banks', was up in a flash. 'Please Miss, nigh to bustin!' She is in her late nineties now, still alive, and she's got a small computer. Miss Blanche Bott, now living in Abbeyfield at Keswick. A great character.

"At this time there was the 800th centenary of the Carlisle Diocese, 1133-1933. They had a very fine pageant in Carlisle and another at

Lingholm, Lord Rochdale's place. From Mungrisdale I took two friends, all three of us in pageant costumes, up for rehearsals. We must have looked a bit odd, sitting in the two-seater Morris, I being in full canonicals as a bishop, with all my robes and things, holding the wheel. The lady sitting next to me was dressed as a reverend abbess and the lady in the back, her daughter, dressed as a very charming court lady, appearing as a princess in the story of St. Kentigern. As we got into Lord Rochdale's grounds I heard a little phut-phut behind me, and glanced round. I saw a motor-cycle. There was a rider and a pillion passenger dressed in wolf skins and woad. Ahead there was a large notice up, 'NUNS ARE REQUESTED NOT TO SMOKE IN THE SHRUBBERY'. A real mixture of ancient and modern! Fifty years later, at a celebration for the 850th anniversary of the diocese, I was speaking to the then Bishop of Carlisle, Bishop Halsay. I said 'I remember the previous one when I brought people from Mungrisdale, and that was the occasion when I was Bishop of Carlisle.' He looked a little startled and said 'Well, I wish I had known for I might have handed this work on to you.' In this later pageant I was Bishop Appleby from sometime in the middle of the 15th century.

"I've never really looked around for another living during my ministry - again, suddenly, something happened. When things came suddenly out of the blue I felt there was some kind of leading. I was now given the opportunity of the living of Loweswater. I was to be there for eleven years, eleven happy years. It has the little lake of Loweswater at one end of it and Crummock at the other end. The fells are all round it, really lovely, and the big hills seen from my window two thousand eight hundred feet. I had two fine church wardens at Loweswater; one of them, Wentworth Robinson, whom everyone called Wenty, the other was George Hope. Everyone was fond of Wenty, a real character. His wife helped to get the Mothers' Union re-started. It evidently had been held every fortnight. In those days they weren't used to farmers' wives going out much and leaving them. The bishop's wife suggested the meetings be held once a month instead of every fortnight and it worked. It was a lovely little church at Loweswater. The congregation was perhaps a little bit bigger than Mungrisdale, but not much. Again it was a farming area, eight miles out from Cockermouth which let me and my wife visit my parents, now a bit nearer, which was quite pleasant. By now I had a 1934 Morris Minor which cost the vast sum of £90.

"At this time my mother gave me a present of a new bicycle. I had a bike which was just not right, just a bit too forward in the frame. There was a man working for me who had worked for the post office. He went back to the post office after he left me. Well, I gave him my bike as I was about to get a new one. He had an ancient bike of his own which I rode the eight miles into Keswick to fetch my new one. It was the most dangerous journey of my life. His name for that bicycle was Rattling Rupert. After the journey I knew why. The bicycle I got in 1936, I am still riding.

"At Loweswater people worked together and got things done. There were the usual characters among them. There was a man who worked, more or less, as the parish clerk. He also helped at the local inn. He would do his washing and dry it in the boiler room of the church. I remember Wenty Robinson had been complaining about something this man had done, I said to Wenty 'Well, after all Wenty, you can't expect to put a quart in a pint pot.' It touched his sense of humour, for Wenty wouldn't have minded a pint! Even after that he'd refer to this man as 'the pint pot'. An example of how people liked Wenty concerned the daughter of Mr Stag who owned a local inn. She was just sixteen and one of the leading lights of the Girls' Friendly Society. They were having their annual party. Wenty had just turned fifty. She said 'Lets ask Mr Wenty, it'll be a better party if he comes.' The younger folk loved him and the older folk trusted him. Looking back I think Wenty Robinson was a man who stuck very much in my mind. In the course of his work as an agent he'd meet folk in the pub, but when it came to Lent he never touched a drop for six weeks. A fine man.

"The other warden, George Hope, was also an outstanding man. It's interesting how ordinary people have such qualities. You find them all over Cumbria. George, a farmer, was a Cumbrian who had come back from Canada. He made the first tractor in the parish out of an old Morris, and it worked well. He organised the farmers' sons and farm lads, got the stones and built the wall when we were extending the church cemetery. We all worked on that together. These two men were a grand pair of wardens.

"I started scouts in Loweswater. A little boy looked over the hedge one day. I said 'You've got a long way to walk to school, haven't you?' The little face looked again over the hedge and said 'There's six of us, Sir.' So I couldn't do anything about it. Or rather I did do something. That was the start of the scouts.

"Then, after eleven happy years at Loweswater, again out of the blue and to my surprise I was offered the living at Muncaster. It was later I heard what had happened. Old Sir John Ramsden of Muncaster Castle had been talking to the rural dean. Sir John had been a cousin of the original Penningtons and the Ramsdens and Penningtons are intermarried. His daughter and her husband are owning the castle now. The rural dean, years and years before, had been my father's curate. I hadn't a clue how he ever thought of me. Anyway he put my name forward and, as in previous livings, since it had come out of the blue I thought I should go.

"During an induction service to the new charge, the incumbent has to ring the bell. This is to let the parish know he has now taken over the duty. We've got a kind of superstition, in this county at any rate, that the new man will probably stay about the same number of times as he rings the bell, the same amount of years. If he only rings it four or five times it's a poor do, but if he rings it twenty or thirty times he'll maybe stay ten or fifteen years, or maybe more. I must have given it a good ring for I stayed thirty years.

"There was a young man in the parish, a Roman Catholic, who was always ready to give a neighbour a hand. He was always doing little jobs for the church. I said to him 'Look here, George, it's time you sent a bill in to the church for these jobs.' He said 'I'll tell you what it is, Mr Hodges, you can give me £200 when you sell your church!' He told me 'The tong has all rusted away on that bell, but I found a nice bit of stainless steel and I put it in. I need a clapper. Do you think this will do?' He fished in his pocket and brought out a two or three pounder cannon ball which he found on the beach. 'Do you think it will do?' A cannon ball ringing a church bell sounded a bit original. He did the job. No doubt it had come from the smuggling trade, but it is now canonised!'

"When I came to Muncaster I wondered what I should do as my predecessors had been 'higher' churchmen than I and had worn the vestments. They were there with all the fancy things. I thought 'Well, if it in some way helps them to worship, it mightn't hurt anybody if I learned how to put them on.' Opinion varied. At the Church Council one fine old sea-captain, Captain Lewellyn, said 'H'm, personally I don't know the difference between a hassock and a cassock.' Walter Marchant the estate agent, a friend, leaned across to him and said 'You sit on the hassock and the cassock sits on you.'

"I encouraged the start of a dramatic society. My virtue is I can learn my lines and remember them. I could learn pretty fast if someone was ill. We also had a choral society. There was a very keen Mothers' Union with plenty of activities going on.

"Muncaster was not only the castle and the estate, it was the parish. Ravenglass, where my wife and I are now retired, is the village in the parish, also it's the postal address.

"A Mr Ogilvy, the agent to the estate, came to Muncaster from Scotland for a little bit. He did a lot for the musical society. His second daughter who had never been south of the Border - she was only six - said 'Daddy, will the English be black?' She discovered we weren't. Mr Ogilvy was the son of Will Ogilvy, the Border poet whose works still sell in Selkirk where the family farm is above the town. Mr Ogilvy is now living in retirement at Seascale.

"In 1951 for the Festival of Britain we had a pageant at the castle and the schoolmistress and I wrote three scenes each. It was a wonderful day and about eleven thousand came. Ravenglass had been an old smuggling place and many of the scenes concerned this area. One lady taking part spread out her skirt over brandy kegs to hide them from the excise men. My wife worked hard for the pageant. Her father was a Cumbrian and her mother was Yorkshire. Her father was Vicar of Thwaites. She was there for thirty-one years, so we were both involved with the church in Cumbria. My wife went to school at Kirkby Lonsdale where Charlotte Brontë was once a pupil, but she has spent most of her life in this area. We've always had teamwork together. My wife was Secretary of the Church Council for twenty-five years. She played the organ for twenty years. She was always involved in the Mothers' Union and over these last years, until they got a vicar's wife to do the job, she filled-in to help there. She ran the Wolf Cubs and was District Commissioner for the Millom area. I was Scoutmaster here well into my sixties. So you see it was a husband and wife commitment to the parish of Muncaster.

"I have a few humorous memories of my days at Muncaster. I had been taking two ladies in my car to Millon to re-license the Parish Hall so that we could have plays and concerts in it. King George VI had just died and Elizabeth was about to be crowned. The idea of an Elizabethan era had been running in people's minds. The magistrate, who must have been nearly as old as I am now, got quietly to his feet and said 'Before we begin our proceedings this afternoon, let us stand in silent memory to King Edward VI.' Truly a magisterial inaccuracy!

"Two days later I was running home some of the Girls' Friendly Society in the car. As I ran the last of the girls home, her name came into my mind and it suddenly struck me 'Elizabeth on the throne and I'm running Mary Stuart home!'

"In 1955 I was elected District Councillor for eighteen years. I was forty-one years in the Parish Council and twenty years a Governor of the local comprehensive school at Millom. I was eighteen years officially as Rector of Waberthwaite Parish. The tithes for Waberthwaite amounted to five guineas. The Penningtons didn't take them, they went to the church, and as I was Rector of Waberthwaite it made me, to my intense surprise, a Lord of the Manor. Waberthwaite was a simple 12th century church. They added the belfry and two bells in 1796 at a cost of £4.10/-. In the early days people would get out their scythes to cut the churchyard grass. We got a Flymo later but I stuck to the old scythe.

"People would do things without being asked. They did things in a good-hearted amateurish way. There were two ladies, Janet Irwin and one of the Mrs Prestons, who tried hard to get the Scouts accounts to come out accurately. But they would not come out by about 1/10d. Finally, as Janet told me, Mrs Preston leant wearily back in her chair and said 'At any rate it's summat similar.' It was near enough!

"Cumbrians are a fine people, perhaps more reticent than some others. They don't push themselves forward in the wrong sort of way. There's a great sense of hard work and steady commitment. One lady my wife and I knew, was Archbishop Ewbank's grandmother who should have been in the Guinness Book of Records. She taught in Sunday-school for eighty-two years!

"Someone who was reading my hand once at the seaside said I'd be an engineer and I ought to wear red. I've generally worn green when not in clerical clothes and I've never become an engineer. I'm no good at all with a spanner. I loved driving bikes, motor-bikes and cars, but when it comes to the mechanical parts of a car I'm no good. A Lancashire friend once saw me handling a spanner and he said 'Ay, we call it in Lancashire cackhanded.'

"I've thoroughly enjoyed my work with the Church schools and I was lucky in having good schoolmasters and mistresses. The state, of course, contributes seventy to eighty per cent of the costs. One is responsible for the fabric and playground and that sort of thing. There are six managers and in a Church-aided school, four of these are connected with the Church, appointed either by the Church Council or the diocese.

"I had some humorous experiences when I myself, taught on certain days at Muncaster and Haberthwaite. I taught the eight to elevens. At Muncaster there was an older boy who had great difficulty with reading and writing. The lesson was on the Roman Wall.

Now I've mentioned Mr Ogilvy, the agent, he thought under the old regime things had got a bit slack. He brought in a Mr Irving from Scotland to pep up the forestry and a head gardener, Mr Blair. At any rate Irving and Blair, were making the old gang work harder than they had done for a bit. How people talk before children and say things without thinking. The headmistress turned to the children and said 'Now children, why did the Romans build that great wall from Carlisle to Newcastle?' This boy put up his hand in a flash, 'Please Miss, to keep the Irvings and the Blairs out.' Ailsa Irving, as the Old Book says, went scarlet with mortification and Jean Blair nearly fell off her chair laughing.

"At Haberthwaite, I thought during a lesson to get in something about Napoleon's last words which were in St. Helena - 'The Almighty was too strong for me' - but I found they had never heard of Napoleon; they hadn't got so far in their history lessons. One little boy said 'Please, I've got him on a cigarette card, he married Mary Louser.' That was the nearest he got to Princess Marie Louise of Austria. That was his translation!

"I retired on the 29th October 1975 after a full and happy life as a minister. We had a nice little party. One tall farmer - we used to be number one and number two on the parish table tennis team - made a speech and said 'Well, when he first came here Mr Hodges was an old young man, now he's a young old man.' My wife and I live happily in Ravenglass with many memories of Cumbria and its people."

MARY NOLAN

Postmistress

"My house and post office are all one and I've lived and worked here as postmistress for thirty-six years in this small village of Boot in Eskdale. I know everybody here and they know me.

"My maiden name was Massicks. I was born just down the road. The first entry in the church registry was in the 1600's on my mother's side of the family. She was a farmer's daughter and most of the family lived in the valley. My father was the head gamekeeper for Sir John Ramsden who owned Muncaster Estate and most of the farms. Father had to organise pheasant shoots and grouse shoots. So I'm very much a country woman and almost the only one left here. Nowadays most of the folk coming to this part of the world are strangers whereas we've been here for over three hundred years.

"We lived in the gamekeeper's house in a lovely spot in the woods by the river, just about a mile from here. There were six of us, three girls and three boys. Mother used to take visitors and we helped her in the house. Father was very hardworking and he made us work too.

"I left to work as a cook in Nelson in Lancashire. Then I went as a nurse to the hospital in Manchester. After that I worked in the uniform factory during the war at Cleator Moor near Egremont. It was there I met my husband, who died in 1950. I've been a widow for thirty-seven years. My only daughter, who is now a deputy head teacher of a school in London, has been a great support and comfort to me.

"I became a postmistress in 1952. We had come to live in Boot just next door to the old postmistress and became friendly with her. She was seventy-eight and had a fall and fractured her wrist. She didn't want to go to a home so I looked after her. I came to live here and she lived for two years.

"At that time we had no electricity and no water and I had to go down to the River Whilan to get our water and carry it back. It was a stony track and when the snow was on it, it wasn't easy. I used oil lamps and candles for lighting.

"The old postmistress was very eccentric. She refused to hand in her resignation till she had completed thirty years as a postmistress.

44

She really wasn't fit and I was in fact doing the job; so when I became postmistress I didn't find that difficult. The head postmaster used to come out to try to persuade her to give in her notice, but she wouldn't. She had actually been in Boot sixty years. It wasn't without its funny side. She had lived in Boot all these years and latterly had got very deaf. One day she kept the doctor waiting about half an hour in the shop because she hadn't heard him, and when he protested she gave him the rough edge of her tongue. Another time she told off Professor Joad when he visited the area. She was eccentric but I liked the old lady and I missed her when she died. Her father had been postmaster before her and then she took over.

"There wouldn't be one hundrd folk in the Boot area then and in winter it was just the locals who came in. I sold newspapers. When I started the old lady sold nothing, there was only the post office. I began to sell groceries, chocolate, ice cream and gifts and anything I could get that was needed. I haven't got a grille like most post offices and sometimes people would come into my little shop and ask 'Where is the post office?'

"For the first thrée years folk could get stamps, postal orders and pensions. Then later came the Savings Bank, and then the Giro Bank and television licences.

"In summer you would get people from all over the world, some living in the hotels and farms. People came to tne C.H.A. - the Co-operative Holiday Association place just down the road. Nowadays I think it's called Countrywide Holiday Association. So in summer the post office was almost a kind of information centre for people from all over the place. You met all kinds of situations, some quite funny and others more serious. One visitor said 'I think I'm going to pass out' and she collapsed on the floor. I got help to take her up and into the sitting room and brought her round and gave her a cup of sweet tea. Then you'd get some comical request like another person who wanted me to sell her a stamped addressed envelope, and another who wanted to buy second-hand stamps!

"Prince Richard of Gloucester was a visitor. He was at Cambridge University at the time and friendly with a boy who came on holiday to Eskdale. A party of lads would come climbing with them, climbing on Scafell.

"The post comes here from Seascale. When I started here the postman had a walking round. He'd go to Ghyll Bank and Birkerth-waite. He'd leave here about ten o'clock and return about half-past one. He'd have chats with people at the farms and around.

"I went to school just down the road. We'd use slates and the slate pencils made scratchy sounds on them. I well remember my old teacher, Miss Armstrong, who of course is dead now. Her parents kept the Woolpack Hotel up the road and she lived there. My aunt was the infant teacher there for a little while.

"There are some visitors you particularly remember. One family kept coming for about twelve years. They had a little girl who would come in and sit in the shop with me and watch everything that was going on. She would be about three at the time and she came till she was sixteen. She took a great interest in the customers. Later when she was a bit bigger she used to help serving lollies and things. I loved that little girl and missed her when she went.

"I suppose it was a great help, being brought up in the country, for working in a country post office. Anybody coming to a tiny community like this from a big town wouldn't have the same feel for a situation like this. It's because in some ways the post office here is more than just a post office. As I said before it is a centre, an information centre for all sorts of questions: where places are, how long does it take to get there - e.g. where Scafell is. Van drivers are for ever coming in and asking where this or that farm or place is. If you've always been part of the area you can help them.

"As time went on I've seen the post office doing more and more things, like rail cards and milk tokens and traveller's cheques. Things seem to keep piling up. But you can always cope because even at a time like Christmas, although it is busier, there are relatively few people in the area. There are so many holiday cottages and many are only occupied in the summer. Then it's really busy because there are so many visitors with the little station just down the road. The Ravenglass-Eskdale railway makes a big difference to Boot for it seems to get busier and busier each year. The railway has got a lot of publicity on television and that brings people.

"Our little school closed and was made into a holiday centre. A school from Workington has control of it and they bring their children out to it during the summer and also they let it, perhaps to a youth club. A school, like a post office, is very important to a village and it's sad when one closes. The post office authorities intend to make this what they call, I think, a community post office, but I won't be postmistress then, I'll be retired. It will only be open two days a week, for three hours on a Monday or Tuesday and three hours on Thursday. I suppose that's better than being closed completely but there are other places where, when the school and post office close, the village life seems to die.

"Looking back it's been an enjoyable life here. There are times in everybody's life which are better than others, but overall it's been a happy time. I've had and made lots of friends, many as tiny tots then as proud mothers and grannies. When people ask me what I'm going to do in my retirement I say 'I'm going to be thoroughly lazy for a bit, then I'll have to think about it.' My roots are here. There are things in church in memory of my ancestors and I've got a deed saying than an ancestor of mine sold the land for this house to be built on. The church register shows that the family, who were yeoman, goes back hundreds of years. On the Massicks side my brother found in a London library that there was a coat of arms for the family.

"Several years ago there was someone from London doing research for the programme "This Is Your Life." They were doing the life of a postman up here who had to retire early because of ill health. He used to be the postman here and he had been very friendly with the old postmistress who had died. They wanted to know all about the different jobs and things at that time so I told them all about them. They said 'We want you to come to London for the programme.' I said 'No,' but in the end they persuaded me to go and I had a lovely time with the postman and his wife. Eammon Andrews was a very nice man and I was sorry to read of his death. There was another time when the radio people came to ask me all about the post office and this area.

"The life of a postman is also different nowadays. The post is now done by mail van from Seascale and he delivers all the way up here and we don't get our letters till about half-eleven. Then another van comes up in the afternoon to collect all we've got, at about a quarter to four.

"Many people who have come to these parts have told me they think it is the best of all the areas. They have Scafell and a most beautiful Eskdale. There are fell walks, but there are also many gentle walks. Families come with children and can walk and picnic by the rivers. Thousands have come from Lancashire. I think British Rail run an 'all in' trip from Morecambe and other places.

"I mustn't forget the wildlife, that is of great interest to many people. You can see the wild fox, the badger, sometimes a deer leaping over a hedge right in front of you, and of course many small animals like the rabbit. Yes, Eskdale is well worth visiting. It is the place where I have my roots and where I've spent many happy years as the village postmistress at Boot."

RALPH CANNON

Reservoir Keeper

"I was born in 1901 and went to the British School in Castle Street, Kendal. I was brought up on a farm about a mile out of Kendal, called Jenkin Crag. I worked on the family farm till I was twenty-nine, then a job was advertised for the Kendal Corporation for a reservoir keeper up at Fisher Tarn. I applied and got the job.

"The old farm was much different from farms nowadays, with no machinery and things done by hand. I used to go to the potato market in Stramongate in Kendal every Saturday. There would be about fifty of us selling potatoes and vegetables. We charged 6d a stone for potatoes. I'd take in about 100 stone of potatoes on the cart and sell the lot in a day.

"There was the reservoir at Fisher Tarn and also two smaller reservoirs at Birds Park that had to be looked after. In the morning I'd go to Fisher Tarn and then down to Birds Park to take the levels of water in them. I had the meters to read at the chlorination plants. The meters registered the water that supplied Kendal. I had to report each day how much water had been used and sent in the report to the Gas and Water Department who, in those days, were responsible for the water supply. Later, when gas was nationalised, I had to report to the borough surveyor. He was my immediate boss. I was there for thirty-six years and until the last four years in the job I was under the Lakes and Lune Water Board. Now it's the Cumbrian Water Board.

"One of my jobs was to attend to the stone walls which ran round the reservoirs. They kept coming down, especially in hard frost, and always needed repair. I must have repaired hundreds and hundreds of yards of stone wall. I just used the fallen stones. You can't just do it anyway. There's a knack in dry stone walling.

"Then I had to go round the runners that fed the reservoirs to make sure there was nothing in them that shouldn't be. I remember one bad incident in one runner. One morning I went to Birds Park. I saw a number of men working there. It was the Manchester people relining the culverts of their pipe-line, the Thirlmere supply to Manchester. They were cementing with compressors and they were working in the culvert just above us. One of our runners came off the fields into a cement basin. It was full of diesel, absolutely full of it. I hurried down to the reservoir and all round it you could see the diesel. I went back and said to the foreman 'You didn't say anything to me about diesel.' He said 'I didn't see it.' I said 'I'm going up to those men who are working up there to see what they're playing at.' I went up and said to them 'What have you been doing? My reservoir is full of diesel!' They said 'Have you reported it?' I said 'Not yet, but I jolly well will do it soon.' I reported it to the borough surveyor who came and met me. Evidently they had had an air-lock in a pipe that was going along the fields. To get rid of the air-lock they had opened this pipe and all the diesel in it had gone straight into our runner and into the reservoir. Their foreman came down and put a match to it. The fire singed the trees beside the reservoir.

"Dr Madge who was in charge of the health problems of the Westmorland water supply asked me to meet him in the morning. This concerned another bit of trouble with these men. They had a toilet near where they were working. Instead of using this toilet, they went into the wood and used that. Dr Madge from Public Health set about putting that right. He was furious and said 'They come here to Westmorland and do what they jolly well like. They're not supposed to go anywhere near the wood.' He contacted Manchester Corporation. There was an awful row and Manchester Corporation settled that problem. Dr Madge, who used to come up to inspect the reservoirs, said to me 'There's nothing to beat your water supply.

"It was a responsible job looking after Fisher Tarn and Birds Park. Fisher Tarn is sixty acres with one hundred and twenty-five million gallons when full. I ran it out of Fisher Tarn into Birds Park and then onto Kendal. But I also supplied the high parts of Kendal town from Fisher Tarn. Nowadays Kendal is supplied from Thirlmere. I also had to keep an eye open for leaks. I went round each morning to measure them. I had a three gallon bucket and I had to time how long it took for the leak to fill the bucket. There was one bad leak that filled the three gallon bucket in three seconds. I had to dip it into the leak and pull it out almost immediately. I had to report just how much leaking there was and the borough surveyor arranged the repair.

"From time to time I had to have men up to help me with certain jobs. Every Friday afternoon I'd have to go down to Birds Park. I had to take the big strainers out and wash them and I needed help because they were so heavy. The strainers would catch any mossy material, also crayfish which could block taps so I had to keep them out of the main. Of course we'd put trout into Fisher Tarn and that gave me another job, for people could apply for permits to fish and I had to check their permits.

"An important part of the work was to look after the chlorination of the reservoirs. That really started during the war when they were afraid the Germans might try to contaminate the water in British reservoirs. After that they were very fussy about it. There was a sample taken each month and the report sent to the Public Health Doctor for Westmorland. I had to see the chlorination plants were working right. They were quite a headache. One element was liquid and the other chlorine gas. If there was a gas leak I had to take a deep breath, run in, shut it off and run out again. You poured the liquid chlorine into a tank and measured it by the bucketful. You had to get the right balance with the two. There was a meter for the liquid. The faster the meter went, the more liquid went into the main. If I got a drop of it on my overalls, it would take the dye out of them. The gas was more of a problem to me. It used to take my breath away.

"One thing that used to bother me was having to tell people they could not get access to certain areas. I'd tell them they should really go to the manager at the gas works and complain to him if they felt they were being shut out, as he was my boss and I had to obey his orders.

"I'll tell you why rules had to be made. Down in London they had been pumping water out of a well. One of the workmen, instead of going to a nearby toilet, was caught short and unfortunately he was a carrier of typhoid and there was an epidemic because of the incident. The result was people working on water supply had to give samples for analysis. Men in Kendal area working on mains had to do it as well. Even fishermen at Fisher Tarn had to do it before they were allowed access. That's why I had to stop the public from getting access.

"During my time there had been no accidents at Fisher Tarn although sometimes dangerous jobs had to be done. There was the big dam to hold the water back. When ice covered it men had to stand on the wall with a large piece of wood which they let drop on the ice, to try to break it up along the dam. The boss thought the ice was putting pressure on the dam. It was quite dangerous. They used a big log of wood like a beam with a ring at each end and a rope. They'd let it drop and then pull it up and move along the dam which was over one thousand feet. There was a wall a few feet wide, they stood on that and could have fallen straight down onto the ice. They had to have a good head for heights. A gang of men worked on this with me in charge.

"Before the war I'd get gangs of men up to drag for weeds at the bottom of the reservoir. They had a big boat and they used ropes with hooks to drag up sheets of weed. I always remember one day when we were pulling this weed in, one of the men burst out laughing and his plate flew out of his mouth, but luckily it dropped onto the weed and he grabbed it just in time.

"Another funny incident I remember was in 1933 when the dam was being repaired. We had a firm from Kendal doing the top seven feet. A cementation company from Yorkshire came to repair the rest with these air compressors. The water was let down of course. They dug the cement out from the stones and forced cement back in again with the compressors. Now at that time there was a swan on the reservoir which was a bit of a nuisance. I'll tell you more about this swan later. My wife used to bake bread for it. It would eat five loaves of bread a week. At this time it was messing about where these men were working and the foreman got a bit fed up with it. He was using one of the compressors. The swan came right up to him and he just stuck it underneath the swan with a full blast of compressed air. It took the bird straight up in the air, oh, three times as high as this house and it was flapping like mad with the compressed stream of air underneath it. It kept it up for a minute or two, then flopped back into the water. It cleared off and I never saw that swan anymore. It had had enough.

"The same swan was involved in another incident before this. An old gentleman from Arnside had come up to fish in the tarn. He was fishing with minnows and he was kneeling down to a can with his back to the water when the swan saw him. Luckily I was coming along the wall. The swan took off, made a bee-line for the fisherman and landed on the old gentleman's back. I had dealt with this swan before. It was flapping and pecking the back of his neck. I had to come round the end of the dam and I ran as hard as I could. I managed to get it off him and into the water. I took him into the house till he was more like himself and recovered. I had taken that swan by the neck before when it had given me a bit of trouble when I fed it. That's how I got it off the fisherman. I took it by the neck and dragged it off him.

"We lived up at Fisher Tarn, my wife and son and daughter. We were very interested in the natural life of the country all round the reservoir. We had the Canadian geese come in winter, also great northern divers, teal and all kinds of ducks. There were foxes that used to go for my hens and rabbits and hares.

"I had a five acre field that went with the job. I had one milk cow and, of course, calves. We made our own butter and I've still got the little glass churn for the cream. I looked after the hens. I used to get up fairly early in the morning to attend to them before my work started. I had an incubator for my own eggs and the chickens were hatched out, the pullets kept for laying and we'd kill and sell the cockerels when they were sizeable. My boss, the gas manager, used to like them and I'd take him one every week. My wife was a member of the W.I. at New Hutton about two miles from Fisher Tarn. We went to church there.

"I've enjoyed my work as reservoir keeper. I had a boss but I was free to make my own decisions about the jobs that came along each day. I've enjoyed my retirement, now about twenty years. I've a big garden and I like gardening. I grow fruit and my own jams, raspberry, blackcurrant and so on. I make a lot of fruit pasties too. My wife died about four years ago. With all its problems it's been a good life. I've been happy in my job."

CONSTANCE GATE

District Nurse

"I was born in 1909. There were seven of us in the family, including Mum and Dad, and we had a very happy life. Mum and Dad were lovely. My father was a Weights and Measures Inspector. I used to have great fun with my brother who was the eldest boy, I was the youngest girl. I would aggravate him out of mischief. He had a girlfriend, whom he eventually married, and her maiden name was Herring. When her letters came for him I used to get them and say 'Miss Fish has written to you,' and he used to be furious with me. I was only about nine or ten at the time and he used to say to Mother 'Hide them when the postman comes and don't let her see them.' But it was all good fun.

"I got married in 1940 and my husband was a Cumbrian bred and born. I've lived here in Maryport ever since. My husband had a gents' outfitters business in the main street that his father had before him. But his heart was never really in the business. He was a historian and model engineer, a real perfectionist who always wanted to be working with his hands. When he left the secondary school his father wanted him to go into the business but he became an apprentice at Mr Wharton's foundry down by the docks.

"Mr Wharton was a very great friend of Dick's father. One day his father said 'If you're not coming into the shop, you can get a job in the Westminister Bank.' It was next door to the shop. He had a fortnight in the bank but, although he was capable of the work, he hated it. So he went down to Wharton's foundry and got a job as an apprentice. He went back to his father and said 'Can I please have a boiler suit, Father?' 'Why?' asked his father. He replied 'I've got a job as an apprentice with Mr Wharton.' His father got two boiler suits down and said 'My lad you'll pay me a shilling a week till they're paid for.' Dick was happy and thought he'd got off quite lightly.

"Later, when the slump came, he got a good job in electrical engineering for he was a gifted man who had been good at science at school. He might well have been an architect for he was good too at designing; I've got his paintings round the walls of my room here.

"In the early days before I married, when there were no vacuum

53

cleaners and washing machines and Mother had her hands full, it was decided I should stay at home and help. I didn't like it. Then a friend of mine who was in the St. John's Ambulance Brigade invited me to come along and Father and Mother allowed me to go. I loved it from the minute I went. It was called the V.A.D.'s in those days. So I went to the infirmary to do voluntary work. I now realised I wanted to be a nurse and nothing else. My father warned me it was hard work and I wouldn't get much pay, but my mind was made up. A nurse I'd be. I'd even stop in the infirmary till nine or ten at night and I wouldn't have minded stopping all night. Father and Mother were getting worried. What was I doing out till that time of night? One day Father said 'You know, they won't give you a gold chain for what you are doing. Do you really want to be a nurse?' Later Mother said 'Do you really want to leave home?' I said 'Well, Mother, I do want to be a nurse.' She said 'Your father and I have talked it over, so if you really want to, you can.' After that I couldn't get going fast enough, before they changed their minds!

"I wrote to the hospital and they sent me an application form. It had to be signed by my parents. At first I didn't tell Father. I let him have his tea before I told him. I was sitting at the bottom of the table, for we were in seniority. I said 'Father, would you please sign this form for me?' 'What form's this?' He put his specs on. 'You've made up your mind? You're quite sure?' 'Yes Father.' I can see him now. He took a fountain pen and I've never forgotten the words he said to me and they really helped me many and many a time when I could have thrown it all up. He turned to me and said 'Remember, my dear, if they don't want you, we do.'

"I did my midwifery and fever training. I got experience all over the place, in Huddersfield, then as a night staff nurse in Worcester. One of the girls I trained went to Hammersmith and we kept in touch. She said 'Why don't you come down and we can have good times together?' So I went to Hammersmith and got my district nurses's training for about two and a half years. Then I went to Devon as a district nurse, then to Gillingham in Kent.

"Dick, my husband, met me through my other brother who was a great sportsman. One night he said 'Mother, can I bring Eleanor to supper?' Now Eleanor was Dick's sister. I didn't know Dick then, though I had heard a lot about him. By now I was seventeen. John, my brother, said 'Oh he's a nice boy is Dick.' One day I was in the house alone. there came a knock at the door and there was this smart young man, well-dressed, smart jacket, chamois leather gloves. He said

'Does John Bolton live here?' 'Yes.' 'Can I speak to him?' 'Sorry, he's not in.' I said 'Are you Eleanor's brother?' And do you know what he said? 'Yes, have you any objections?' Later, when my sister Kathleen came in, I told her about Dick's visit and she asked 'What is he like?' I said 'He's a stuck up little thing.' That was how I met Dick and that was before I set out on my nursing career.

"He was visiting again one night when I was upstairs trying on my new nurse's uniform. When I came downstairs he looked at me in surprise and said 'What are you wearing that for?' I told him I was going to be a nurse. When he had gone Mother said, 'Has he been saying anything to you?' I said 'No, why?' 'Well, he said a most peculiar thing when you went upstairs. He turned to me and said 'Mrs Bolton, I'll never marry a nurse.'

"Years later he wrote to me when I was an assistant matron in Huddersfield. When I opened the letter it had a lot of postcards in it, all views of Maryport and the district. He described them all on the back and he wrote 'I'd like to show you these myself.' That was how it started and how I came to be in Maryport. We were married on November 30th 1940. By that time Dick had taken the shop over. His father had died and his mother pleaded with him as she didn't want the business to go out of the family. He also volunteered for the fire brigade and was kept very busy.

"One night a lady came and introduced herself as Miss Illingworth, the Superintendent of District Nurses from Carlisle. She said she'd heard I'd done a lot of district nursing, one of her nurses had had a major operation and she'd be off months and could I help her? I asked Dick and he said 'It's up to you.' Miss Illingworth suggested I might do part-time. Even that would help her. Well, I started by helping three days a week, then it got to a week, then doing holiday duties. The superintendent came down from Carlisle and said 'Mrs Gate, I've been looking at your worksheet. Do you realise you're putting in more hours part-time than the full staff nurses?' I said 'I've been happy and it suits me.' She said 'Well I think you're very foolish. I realise there's room for another nurse in Maryport. You're not getting holidays with pay and you're not getting a pension. So you think about it.' By then I had two girls growing and I asked my husband again and he said 'It's your job and you understand it.' I thought 'Well, I could give it up if it didn't work out.' So I became a full-time district nurse in Maryport.

"When I first started I had to walk everywhere. Then they decided they would buy me a bicycle. After that Dick bought me an autocycle.

I had that for years and they made me an allowance for the petrol,-1¼d a mile. But as I was out in all weathers on the autocycle and often got soaked, I asked if there was a chance of getting a car, and at last I got one.

"My permanent area was Maryport, although sometimes I went beyond it. Maryport used to be a mining port. It was much poorer in those days. There was a fishing fleet when the docks were open. Boats from Spain and other countries came in for coal from the pits which were working. The working class certainly were very hardworking. There was a shipbuilding yard down at the dock, Ritsons Yard. So it was the families of miners, fishermen and townspeople I worked among. There wasn't the poverty I had seen in London and other places. You never saw children without shoes. Difficulties were often due to bad management in the home. There were some parents then, just as now, who didn't care.

"The object of district nursing is to train families as one goes round, to educate them as much as possible in hygiene and making sure children are taken to have their injections against polio. The health visitors used to back us up and we used to back them up.

"We hear today of children being put into care. I had a case where two children were involved. A doctor rang me up to ask if I'd be good enough to visit this house, see an old man in it, give general attention and give the children a bath and put clean clothes on them. I went about five o'clock and it was wintertime. I knocked and knocked on this door but nobody came. I knew I had got the right address. I looked upstairs and there were two little faces at the window, dirty, filthy council house windows. I motioned them to come down and open the door which they did. I asked 'Where is your mother?' They didn't know. I said 'I've come to see a man' and they said 'That's Grandad. He's upstairs.' I went upstairs expecting to see a poorly old man in bed, and there was this man as dead as dead could be. I looked at these children and asked them if they had anything to eat. They really were like pathetic little orphans of the storm. There was some old mouldy bread in the pantry. I looked in the cupboards. There was nothing.

"I went to the lady next door and asked if she knew what was going on. She was a kindly woman who said the mother had gone off the previous day and she'd taken the children in. The grandfather probably hadn't been dead when she left. I told here I'd be back and I rang the NSPCC they said they'd send a man out and what time would I be back? This Doctor Robert Rattray was a fine man. He was killed in a car accident ten years ago. He was an angel, that man, the loveliest doctor, he really cared. When I told him he said 'Oh Nurse Gate, what have I let you in for?' I said my chief worry was for the two children who had been left all night. I told him I had rung the NSPCC. I went back to the house and when the NSPCC officer came he was disgusted: but that was the only time I had children taken away into care.

"There was another one that was a borderline case. A colleague was going away on holiday the week before Christmas and asked me if I would go to a certain lady in Loweswater Road. She couldn't remember the number, but it was only a short little road and I'd recognise the house because the gate was broken off. The woman was pregnant and due any time and her blood pressure had to be taken twice a day. I was on my way to this house when I met one of the doctors. He said 'Have you been to Violet's yet?' 'No, I'm on my way.' 'Oh good,' he said, 'for she has a Christmas present for you.' 'Have you got one?' I asked him. He was laughing, 'You bet I've got one!'

"I found this house with the broken gate, crusts of bread all over the drive. When I got in and looked at the kitchen floor, do you know what there was for carpets? Old army coats that the Home Guard used to wear. I just stood and looked and asked Violet 'What's all these?' She just said 'We hadn't a carpet so I put them down.' It was a council house living-room. The furniture was quite all right. The wallpaper on the walls was beautiful, looked very professional. But on the sideboard was a big goose with its neck hanging down, dripping blood on the floor. (I knew then what the doctor had been laughing at when he joked about a Christmas present.) The middle leaf of the dining table had been taken out and in it were empty tins that had baked beans in and cellophane wrappers that had held bread. The ashes from the grate were right out into the room which had chip papers all over it. You never saw such a mess. She herself was in an awful filthy state.

"I took her blood pressure which was all right. I asked her how old she was. 'Twenty-eight.' I said 'Don't you think you should have made some effort to make the place nicer for yourself and the children?' The two youngsters who were sitting on the settee were really filthy. 'What's wrong with the children?' she asked. I said 'Don't you think they could do with a good bath?' She said 'They had a bath before you came.' I replied 'I'm sorry but that isn't the case. They didn't have a bath. I have two girls and I know when children have had a bath.' I said 'Wouldn't it be nice, as your room is beautifully decorated, to keep the rest of it nice and clean. Who decorated it?' 'My husband, he is a painter and decorator. But it's all right for people like you to talk.' I had quite a job trying to help her to see things right.

"When my colleague came back from holiday and attended the woman again, she rang me up and told me what had happened. An inspector from the NSPCC had called, went upstairs and found filth and exreta on the mattresses. He gave the parents two days to clean it up. The woman did clean it up for she was frightened the children would be taken into care. I never had any trouble with most of the parents who were very nice to me, but you did come across some difficult people.

"I had many many friends in the town and such a lot of them knew my husband. During the years of depression before the war Dick's father, when it was dark, gave Dick a sealed envelope with money in it. He'd say 'Now Dick, I want you to go down street.' He said 'Go to this number where there's a big family and put this envelope through the letter box and try not to let anybody see you.' After his father died people would come into the shop and say 'Many a time when things were hard, your dad gave us our bread and butter.

"What are the qualities needed for a district nurse? I can only repeat what I was told in my training. A nurse must remember she is a guest in someone else's home and she must behave as a guest. If you make the right approach at the first visit, you've won, but if you go in like a bull in a china shop, you've lost. You became sensitive to people and the way they lived. You learned that often you found kindness, sympathy and understanding in some working class homes that was absent in some middle class homes. You learned to sense quickly each house you visited.

"I retired in 1969 after a happy life in nursing. You attended people who are now parents and grandparents. When you were out walking you met someone with a child who said 'Remember him, Nurse Gate? You were the first to see him.' There is a fine continuity in district nursing. The day I retired one of my daughters took my place as district nurse. Wasn't that lovely?"

BOB CLARKE

Farmer, Wrestler, Horn-stick Maker

"My grandfather and father were Westmorland farmers, but farming was much different in grandfather's day. There were no machines then; it was horses and your hands that did the work. I was brought up with horses. They were my great love. We used to have five horses. We actually bred them and they made money for us. We had two mares for breeding. With a bit of luck they bred you a foal each year, so we had two horses to sell each year. We sold them at five years old. That was at Craketrees Farm about twelve miles north-east of Kendal.

"My father took over in 1910. He hadn't an easy time and when I started farming I hadn't an easy time either. There was little spare cash around. In fact, it wasn't till the late 1940's I could afford a tractor. I started on my own in 1940. When I got married we had spent the first year working for my father. I got the princely sum of thirty bob a week.

"At that time Father was tenant at the family farm which was owned by the Pattinson family of Windermere. When he was retiring it fell vacant but I didn't get the chance of that farm, which was a great disappointment to me. But I got a farm of my own just over the hill from here, Bracken Hall, Lammering. The farm I'm in now is Grayrigg Foot near Grayrigg village. The beck that's at the bottom of the garden divides Grayrigg from Lammering. Grayrigg Foot, we believe is the oldest building in the area and there was a farm here in the eleventh century.

"I took over Bracken Hall in 1940. I took it as tenant but I bought it off the landlord in 1953. Then in 1967 I managed to buy this place also - Grayrigg Foot. Then we had the two places with a man helping me. I did the dairy side of the business and used to start at five o'clock in the morning. I had forty-four cows here. I kept young stock and five hundred pigs at the other place and, of course, the sheep.

"The late twenties and early thirties were desperate for men like my father and grandfather. You hear folk say these are bad times now, but no way can you compare them with pre-war. Things began to pick up with the approach of war, but in the late twenties there was

59

no money anywhere and many farmers went out of business.

"I've done all sides of farming, but working with horses and sheep was my favourite. The sheep were Rough Fell, a couple of hundred of them. Sheep were profitable and despite what some folk say, they still are.

"I've made my life interesting by my many interests. Wrestling is one of them - Cumbrian and Westmorland wrestling. You've got to remember that in the old days in this part of the world, wrestling was about the only sport you could take part in. The lads and men employed on the farms, when they finished their work, used to gather at certain parts in the area and wrestle. Everybody would throw a penny each in a cap and there'd be a wrestling knock-out competition, winner takes all. With twenty-four lads that would give you two bob, and that was an awful lot of money in those days. I used to want to be old enough to wrestle seriously. The whole idea was to win. I liked the challenge of it.

"With Cumberland wrestling the rules are different. Whoever is first to touch the ground with any part of the body above the ankle is the loser. Usually it's the best of three tries. The body posture is low down. Behind your opponent's back the fingers of your two hands are not separately intertwined, but are firmly cupped and clasped together. If your fingers were interlocked separately that was an ideal way to get them broken!

"I began to wrestle in the open competitions, then I had a serious accident at work. A runaway horse made an awful mess of my right arm and that was me out of wrestling. As you can still see today, my elbow is twisted and there are lumps all the way down my arm. That's what I got trying to stop a runaway horse. I think this was the biggest disappointment of my life. I tried to take up wrestling again but my arm wouldn't allow it.

"I kept up my interest in the sport and in later years they called me in as a judge. My wife Dorothy is also a judge. In fact she is the only lady member of the sports' governing body - the Cumbrian and Westmorland Wrestling Association - and I've been president of the association these last ten years. A number of years ago I was appointed manager of the wrestling at Grasmere Sports.

"The reason my wife became interested is that wrestling usually runs in families. My father was a great wrestler. Her father was a wrestler, and if you're a wrestler you talk wrestling, it was part of the family conversation. So eventually she got involved, and now she does an awful lot or organising. Today she's down at Morecambe to get competition trophies. Women may go in for all-in wrestling but not for our sport. She is, as I said, a judge, and governing board members have to judge world championships at various meetings all around the North of England and the Scottish border country. People apply and the board has to sort out who should judge particular classes of wrestlers. The classes start with boys under fifteen and there are ten championship classes, up to heavy-weights.

"It's a professional sport with world championships. It's not amateur. You won't make a living out of it, but there's prize money. We've had Germans taking part in the championships, and Austrians. But that's rare. You find people from these parts have emigrated and started the sport overseas. Very occasionally they do come over to wrestle in these events. Championships have been applied for at Annandale, Newcastle, Coniston, Carlisle, Garstang, Millom, the Roman Wall, Ullswater and a few other places.

"At the age of twenty I was wrestling at eleven stones; this was a popular class in those days. We had a local lad who was twenty stones and he was a heavy-weight champion for a number of years. Nowadays when I go to championships I am mostly on the microphone, commentating on the wrestling. I've done it for a few television programmes. I usually like to put a bit of good old Westmorland dialect on, for folks like that. At places like Grasmere Sports and Ambleside, holiday places, visitors like to hear the dialect. There is a difference between the real Westmorland and Cumbrian dialects. I can tell the difference. I'm afraid our dialect is dying out. Perhaps television is helping to bring this about and makes us all a bit more uniform.

"Cornish wrestlers have come up here. But the types of wrestling are different. The hold is different. The Cornish when wrestling wear a jacket. They can grab hold of this jacket and they can use the hands anywhere. Our lads wear long johns, a vest, and what they call a centre piece, just a kind of briefs. A number of the vests are decorated and at a number of the wrestling meets there is a competition for the smartest costume. This is where the ladies come in with fine needlework - the wives, girlfriends and mothers. I have a photo here of a lad from Carlisle who is the most successful wrestler we've ever had, and he's still wrestling at forty-three years of age! It was never known to happen before but he won the eleven stone class, the twelve stone class and the thirteen stone class at Grasmere Sports.

"In my so-called retirement, for I'm now seventy-six, my other interests are horn-stick making and bowling. I got a horn as a gift and

I thought I'd have a go at the stick making. I had no lessons and was just self-taught. Each stick you make you improve on. First of all you boil the horn for about twelve hours to soften it, just in boiling water in an iron pan on the fire. Then stick it in a vice and pull it into some short of shape to start with. You can't get the right shape right off. After that it's a case of using dry heat, gas or blow lamp. You must use it very, very gently so as not to burn it, and that softens the horn. You start with a pretty strong rasp to cut it down for a start. Then a medium rasp, followed by a finer rasp. Use the heat on a little bit at a time and gradually pull it into the shape you want. After that, start with pretty rough sandpaper, then use medium and then use fine sandpaper. When the sandpaper has done its job, get a handful of steel wool and rub away for hours till you get the real glossy finish of the horn. The last thing is to varnish it with a clear varnish. That's the head finished, and the next thing is selecting a pretty straight stick of hazel wood which has been dried for at least two years and you dowel them in to make a perfect fit. Of course I use fine sandpaper on the stick and, if the stick is a wee bit bent, you can straighten it with a little dry heat. I usually use dark oak varnish on the stick.

"I give them to friends, as Christmas presents or for any occasion, and sometimes I sell them to make money for various organisations and sometimes raffle them. I can spend forty hours on making a stick. Of course I do a little bit at a time. You've got to work very carefully. You see, when you heat them to get them into shape you must get the right heat, it should't be too much or too little. You bend them again just a little bit at a time, then let them cool off. So you're not at it non-stop.

"With constant rasping and sandpapering it's not easy. It can be quite a strain on the arm. But it's the pleasure I get out of it that's important. That's really the whole idea. It's really a hobby, for I've still got jobs to do about the farm, fences and so forth, although I've rented out pastures. And of course we've got a lovely big garden to look after.

"Bowling is another hobby, outdoor in summer and indoor in the winter months. We play then in the leisure centre in Kendal. I was sixty-eight years of age when I started bowling. I had never even seen crown green bowling before. I went to this green at Endmoor and watched them play and thought, 'By gum, I'd like to have a shot at that!' Well, they invited me in and straightaway I was enjoying it. I was a year at Endmoor but they weren't in any particular league, and by this time I was improving and wanted to be in a team. I like competition and I couldn't bowl just for the sake of bowling.

"I then joined Burneside and, after bowling there for one year, they called me into the team and I've been in it ever since. By the third year I was in their first team. Put it this way; whatever you're doing, do it to the best of your ability and if you become good, well, that's a bonus. When it comes to matches, if you win, that's another bonus. You've got to put all you've got into it, whether its farming or making sticks or bowling. Last season, in indoor bowling, we won the second division. Next year we're promoted to the first division. Retirement, I think, is the time to do all the things that give you pleasure that you couldn't do during your working life.

"It's been a hard but enjoyable life. When I started farming as a married man, we had less than £500 between the pair of us. This was at Bracken Hall which we rented. The wife furnished one bedroom, and downstairs we had a table and a chair each. From then on we worked to stock up and furnish the house. Our motto was not to buy anything till we could afford to pay for it. I was just made that way. If I had to borrow money I don't think I could sleep. I realise nowadays folk have a different attitude, but for me it has been a good life."

BRYAN STILLING

Mountain Search and Rescue

"I'm a Kendal man and went to the council school in Kendal in Castle Street, called then the British School, a primary school. As a senior boy I left school at fourteen and got a job at K Shoes in 1932, when you were lucky to get a job. I was in the welting section. I joined the Territorials and when war broke out went right in and was in France from the start. When the war was over I came back to K Shoes as an operative and stayed there till I retired.

"When I came out of the army after the war - I had been in the Border Regiment - I took up fell walking. There was a group of us, and when the appeal came from the police at an Easter weekend disaster which involved several deaths, we responded to it. As well as fell walking we had been doing some mountain climbing and pot-holing - I was never very good at rock climbing, but I did a lot of it. When the appeal came, about half a dozen of us at Kendal formed a search team which grew in number. We linked up with the police and got a stretcher and started from there. Like all teams, the movement started with people who had been going on the fells.

"In the early days we called a meeting and we got about twenty-five members in the Kendal team. There are two types of accident: there's rescue when someone has fallen down a crag or somebody's fallen down on on a fell walk, it's a first aid job to get them down on a stretcher to base and on to hospital. That's rescue. Search on the other hand is when someone's gone out and hasn't come back. Kendal is mainly a search team although it has been involved in both types. Today the official name is Kendal Mountain Search and Rescue Team.

"The team has an active membership of around fifty from Kendal and surrounding districts. It's based in a purpose-built garage in Busher Walk. The team carries out a variety of duties, from rescuing crag-fast sheep and searching for lost walkers to assisting at road accidents and helping those in trouble on the fells. In 1987 the team dealt with eighteen incidents and in 1988 it dealt with seventeen incidents in the first six months of the year. More people visit the fells every year and consequently there are more accidents. Team members train every month and are called out as necessary. We may get several accidents in one weekend and then go for several weeks without incident. We are all volunteers and radios and vehicle equipment are all paid for by voluntary subscription.

"Over the years I got more and more involved. In 1954 I had become Secretary of the Kendal Search Team and I was Secretary until I retired. I had gone to the first meeting of the Lake District Mountain Accidents Association in about 1956. I was on the committee and the following year I became Secretary. Then I became the Incident Officer and was also the Incident Officer for N.R.C., the National Rescue Committee for England and Wales, and I'm still doing that. I put out a report once a year. I do the editing of the incidents in the form of the Lake District Mountain Rescue and Search Teams' Magazine Report which is published once a year. We've got permission to use the very nice cover of Gimmer Crag from Mr Wainwright's *Lakeland Fells*.

"I remember an incident on Scout Scar in the Kendal area. This was a chap who collapsed with a heart attack up on the Scar. We put a line search on and found the body. Another time we were involved with a Kendal man who had gone to Grasmere with his daughter. While she was shopping in Grasmere he said he'd go for a walk, but later she couldn't contact him so she rang the police. They called the Kendal team out and they searched from the early evening to about three o'clock in the morning. We searched all the area round Grasmere as he was an elderly chap and probably wouldn't get very far, then we came back to Kendal. When we were coming through the main street I saw an elderly man walking down Finkle Street. We stopped and asked him where he was going. He said he was shopping. We said the shops wouldn't be open for some time as it was only five o'clock in the morning. It was the missing man and he had actually walked from Grasmere back to Kendal. He was confused. Anyway, he was found.

"Another incident that comes to mind was a search up in Kentmere that went on all night. We searched on the paths all the way up and over the area and then down to where the police were based. Usually a police officer would go with you, or they are in touch with you from base. This chap had actually gone home to Lytham St. Anne's without telling anyone. You get a lot of this sort of thing.

"A tragic case was a chap up at Nan Bield. He collapsed and died. His daughter was there. What you've got to do when you find a body is first to identify it; search to find out name and other particulars. You can't move the body till you have brought along a policeman. The daughter was very upset and that was a sad case.

"Perhaps the most dramatic incident was again in Kentmere. A chap had collapsed near the top of Harter Fell, two thousand five hundred feet high. It was the middle of winter with snow about. His companion suspected a heart attack and came down and said he was in a bad way. We discussed it and realised it would take us an hour to get there and get the stretcher up and we'd have to get him down to hospital. So we called in a helicopter. When we got to the top there was a gale blowing and he was on the edge of the ridge. The helicopter came down and hovered two or three feet from the ground. When we got him in under the blades there were only about three inches to spare. We had to risk it to get him in. The chopper was battling against the gale and moving up and down. But we got him off to hospital.

"If you go to the graveyard at Wasdale Head you'll see many tragic tombstones, the results of accidents on the mountains and fells. What happened before the last war was that when a person was hurt, someone would go down and get the local farmers to come and help. But just after the war, about 1946, there was a big upsurge of people coming to the Lakes for the outdoor life and with that came an increase of accidents. There was obviously a need here and local people became involved in going to help those who had been hurt.

"There were two areas where teams of a sort were originally formed and there have been arguments about which was the first. The one was at Coniston and the other at Keswick. In Keswick you had a retired Colonel Westmorland whose father or uncle was the first man to climb the Pillar Rock in 1880. He formed a team in Keswick. In Coniston there was a chap called Jim Cameron who was one of the first rock climbing guides in the Lake District. He formed the team in Coniston. These teams were formed just after the war. They had very elementary equipment.

"Then one Easter, as I mentioned, there was a really bad accident. It had been very bad weather. It started out warm and then the weather changed dramatically during the weekend. A lot of people walking were caught in trouble. There were possibly four people who died from exposure on the hills. The police who were responsible for mountain rescue - they still are - were inundated with calls about people missing. They put out a request on the radio - 'Will anybody who is fell walking or a climber please help in the searches for people and congregate at Ambleside, or any area where people are lost during the weekend.'

"Hundreds came along and it was a bit of a shambles at first for people were going out in all directions, organised in a very elementary way. Anyway as a result of all this - the development was of a typical, spontaneous British-type - teams started on their own initiative. The Kendal team was started in 1954-55 and it was one of a lot of teams which started about the same time - Cockermouth, the two Outward Bound Schools at Eskdale and Patterdale, the one started at Wasdale and so on. The Langdale team which existed was enlarged. As a result of all this nine or ten teams came into being in the Lake District.

"There was a north and south divide going over the Raise, Dunmail Raise, for then you had Cumberland and Westmorland. There was a movement started on the Westmorland side to form an association of teams, the Mountain Accidents Association. This was fairly representative of teams in South Lakeland.

"I've been involved in South Lakeland since the start. I was the Secretary for seven years. Eventually teams from all over the Lake District got together and the Lake District Mountain Accidents Association was formed, embracing all the teams in the Lake District. There is no actual control for each team is autonomous. We meet twice a year. The Association is an umbrella organisation covering the Lake District teams, the Search Panel, police representatives and others interested in mountain rescue such as the R.A.F. and National Park Rangers.

"When an extended search is needed several teams in the area will be called out. There was, for instance, a chap missing. He was working at a hotel in Langdale. He went off for a walk and he didn't come back. They called all the teams in the area on an extended search, weekend after weekend, and it was three months before he was found. This incident indicated there was a need for a better co-ordination on extended searches between teams who were concerned to get better systems of operation.

"There was a meeting called in Keswick of all the teams and we formed the Lake District Search Panel which is part of the Mountain Accidents Association, but a separate part. Their job is, having a list of skilled people, if there's someone missing for twelve hours after the initial team has gone out, they'll get together with the police and decide what to do and what to search and call in other teams as necessary.

"Just imagine if you go for a walk, say on Benson Knott, and you don't return. Somebody will ring the police and the police will call the Kendal team out. They'd first find out what state you were in when you left, what you were wearing, where you intended going and so on. If they didn't find you before nightfall the Search Panel would meet say at Meal Bank, set up headquarters and decide what area to search and how many teams to pull in.

"An example of an extended search was the case of the French girl at Wasdale where teams searched over a wide area but her body wasn't found till nineteen months later. She had slipped and fallen into a cleft and had been killed.

"As well as calling in teams from outside we can call out dog handlers, a separate organisation attached to each team. They train the dogs which have got to be vetted and accepted. And of course we can pull in helicopters which have been used more and more in recent years. If you've got a casualty, say with spinal injuries, and carrying him down on a stretcher is going to make him worse, you can call in a helicopter. Our earliest equipment when we started was a Civil Defence stretcher and a first aid kit.

"The biggest problem at the start was really communications. On the search there was no radio. If you were out on the fells and the casualty had been found, meantime, somewhere else, you'd maybe come back to discover the casualty had been found perhaps just an hour after you had set out! We developed forms of communication like rockets and flares. We got maroons from the coastguards. We even got bren guns using blanks on an exercise with other teams; we got them from the local Territorials. We tried firing them to see how far they would carry, but they didn't carry very far. In the early sixties we got some Japanese walkie-talkie sets. Some teams had army equipment but it was very heavy and sometimes unreliable. Now communications are covered by the police with a very sophisticated control system.

"In the beginning the vehicles were really our own cars. Then came Land Rovers and the teams developed their own equipment. An important development was the capacity to administer hot oxygen to a casualty suffering from exposure, this gets him warm. The hot air machine was developed by a lad on Humberside. Teams can hire these machines. Our teams, although volunteers, are now very professional and as good as any rescue teams in the world.

"It is the police who are ultimately responsible for all operatives connected with search and rescue. Our relationship in Cumbria with the police is extremely good. The police are on our committees and take part in our deliberations. Of course many of them are local lads. We have to remember too the R.W.V.S. who provide a mobile canteen. What happens regarding the police is that when a big search is going on, we have a search panel and on that panel is a policeman, a superintendent or whoever's in charge. It is the panel with a police presence in it which decides what to do. The panel's advice is available to the police and they almost always take that advice. It is a relationship that works well. After all the advice has been given, then the police will call-out, although team leaders who are in the panel help with the phoning. When you're working with the Cumbrian police it's fine; there's no problem.

"I think it's a worthwhile job the Search and Rescue people do. There's a good feeling about the work, much the same as with the Lifeboat Service; it's a proud service with each team aiming to do the very best. My own feeling is that we should try to make things a little better than we found them. We can only do our best."

BLANCHE BOTT

Schoolteacher

"I was born in 1892. My father was a clergyman at Aspatria, in Cumberland, and I was the fourth of twelve children. The family moved to Ousby in the Pennines. Until I was twelve we were taught by our parents at home. I had a good education from them. They taught us, among other things, English, Latin and French.

"When I was twelve a friend of Father's, who was a clergyman at Workington and who had two daughters about my age, wrote to him. He said one of his daughters had gone to college and would Father let one of his daughters come to stay with Mary, the other daughter for company. So I went and at Workington I went to school for the first time.

"When I was sixteen I became a pupil-teacher in Workington. I taught so many days in the week. I got £5 in my first year as a pupil-teacher and £10 in the second year. That was my salary, but it was good training to learn to manage children. We had to prepare a certain lesson which was supposed to last half an hour and the headmistress and other teachers would come to listen and the headmistress would later criticise it. Sometimes at the end of ten minutes the headmistress would say 'That's all.' That was a short half-hour!

"Then, after two years as a pupil-teacher, I went to Whitelands College for teacher training in Chelsea, London, near where the Chelsea Pensioners live. Elsie Green, Mary's sister, had gone to Whitelands in 1906. Then Mary went. She became a teacher. Then I went from 1910 to 1912.

"Whitelands was an interesting college. When it was first established in 1835 its purpose was essentially a place of religious training, not merely to provide instruction. An earlier training centre in Westminister had concentrated too much on instruction. Whitelands believed that developing what they called a body of "truly capital Christian and efficient schoolmistresses" would be an improvement.

"In 1874 a young principal aged thirty-five was appointed. John Faunthorpe was Principal for thirthy-three years. John Ruskin started off the idea of an annual celebration that began with a church service and with a May Queen and crowning ceremony and revels of different kinds. The principal took up John Ruskin's idea. In the years I was there we had Queen Louise, Queen Elsie III and Queen Alice.

"The students themselves used to dress in special white or pastel coloured dresses for May Day. The queens' dresses were first made to fit any student since voting for the queen didn't take place until the actual May Day morning. So the robes had to be simple, flowing, loose-fitting garments which had intricate embroidery. Later they collected measurements from every girl eligible for election before May Day and then had to make a dress specially for the girl who was chosen. Still later the result of the election was announced well before May Day so that the new queen could choose the style of her dress and to have it made to measure. In 1910 Queen Louise had a beautiful dress with a long train.

"We were all inspected when we were ready to leave college. I had always wanted rural teaching and I was first sent to West Yorkshire near Doncaster, a rural primary school with five teachers. I taught pupils from eight and nine upwards. Now the Secretary of the Cumberland Education Authority was a friend of Father's. He heard I was teaching and suggested I should return to Cumberland as a supply teacher. I came back in 1914 and was a supply teacher for four years during the First World War. My salary was £6 a month, a big difference from £5 a year! I went to Great Salkeld, Edenhall, Longtown and to Penrith because they were taking away the men teachers. I taught the bigger pupils at Penrith.

"When I was twenty-three I went to Mungrisdale which was to play a big part in my life, but to begin with I was just one year there as a supply teacher. I was very lonely then as I didn't know people. In 1916 I went again as supply to Lanercost near Brampton. Then in 1920 it turned out that they wanted to appoint a woman back in Mungrisdale. There were people against appointing a woman, but they said as they knew me they would take me. So I returned to Mungrisdale. There was a great prejudice against women as teachers. They preferred men to women because of discipline and they thought we hadn't the brains for such a job. I remember when I was at Lanercost a farmer came to me. His boy was getting on for fourteen and he wanted him to leave. He said 'You won't be able to teach him any more.' He had an idea that I had used up all I knew by the time his boy was fourteen. I said 'If he stayed with me till he was twenty he'd learn a lot more.' They didn't think women were any good as teachers, that we didn't use the stick. I was in Mungrisdale till 1953, until I retired. You might say the little village of Mungrisdale was my life. I was happy there.

"I liked nature study and gardening and they played quite a part in my teaching. The children were country children and after school they would show me birds' nests. The fells were all around us and we had a good garden.

"Mungrisdale, about eight miles from Keswick with Skiddaw rising about three miles away, was in a farming area and we had our joiner and blacksmith. The managers of the school, there were nine, were all people from the area. They were great critics. There was one, a farmer, John Jackson, I would meet on the way to school. He'd say 'You should be teaching the boys more measuring.' You see, they had to measure the stones in those days for road work and so on. He thought I should be teaching more mensuration.

"You got children of different abilities, but when I left every child could read. I was keen to make the 'three R's' understood. My pupils still write to me and that's very nice. The other day I had a letter from a 'boy'. He is now over seventy and had been speaking to another old Mungrisdale pupil. I've just had a letter from Australia from a pupil who is now eighty, one of my oldest scholars. Another brought me in scones and cakes.

"Talking about food, the pupils and I would bring our lunch to school. They would put their potatoes under the fire in the grate in the classroom at nine o'clock and the potatoes would be nicely baked by dinner time. Then we used to make soup. One would bring a big bowl and we'd bring different vegetables. After the Second World War, of course, they started the school dinners and they ate them in school and I supervised them. I was never asked to do it. They just told me I had to do it. The new arrangements pleased the parents. They had to pay 6d a day and I collected the money on Monday mornings. The food came in van from Threlkeld. It came in two big cans and the pupils helped the van man get it in. It meant now I had no break from the children from half-past eight till half-past three. It could be very tiring.

"The children were taught music. We had good concerts every year with the older pupils. We went round with about twenty carolling every Christmas on behalf of the blind.

"In those days there wasn't much time for many special events outside school. You had to devote so much of your time to preparing lessons and to marking all the work the pupils did each day.

"During the war we had evacuees and a teacher came with them.

Before the war I had an assistant teacher who was very good but after the war I was on my own. Before the war I had written direct to Carlisle pointing out than with about fifty pupils a lot of one's energy was devoted to keeping discipline. The managers didn't think an assistant was necessary as teaching was in their opinion an easy job. The Secretary of Education said he knew the managers were against an assistant but he would send me an assistant on supply. They sent me Miss Barnfather who turned out to be an excellent teacher. I had her till the war, then we had the evacuees with their teacher.

"The evacuees came from the Newcastle region. They weren't accustomed to the country' they were very poor and kept their food on the desks beside them because they were afraid one of the others would steal it. The evacuee teacher took the infants in the school and I took the older ones. Some went home very soon as they didn't like living in an isolated village. Parents would come and stay with villagers and farmers at weekends and expect to be fed and kept for the weekend. Some people were against putting up evacuees or their families, others were quite willing. I couldn't take in any myself as my mother was living in my digs in Mungrisdale during the war and there wasn't room.

"I had some promising pupils. I remember one fine girl who went on to be a nurse in London. One snag was that even if a boy did well in his eleven plus exam, the parents didn't want the boy to go off. They wanted the boy to stay in work on the farm. I remember a clever boy from Newcastle who was an evacuee. Now some of these parents were a bit snobbish regarding rural teachers. A clever boy like Johnny wasn't expected to get a good education in a little country school like Mungrisdale. However, Johnny did very well in his eleven plus exam and it was nice of his parents to come to me and say how well he had been taught and how good his English was now. I felt quite pleased about that. Johnny is now a bank manager in Leeds.

"I remember another boy. We weren't supposed to take children from other schools. One day a grandmother came to see me - would I take her grandson who attended another school? His schoolmaster had thrashed him and he wouldn't go back to school. The lad, who was only six at the time, had sworn at his teacher. I talked it over with Miss Barnfather as she would have to teach him. However he did very well with her. He went on to work at their farm and he got married. About a year ago the door of my bedroom opened and a very well-dressed, educated man came in. He said 'You don't know who I am.' This was the boy, Russell Race, now a man of sixty-four, who had come to see me. It was kind of him and I was so pleased with his success in life. He had always sent me Christmas cards but I never expected him to come and see me.

"I get a bit sad when I look at education today. I knew some teachers after I had retired. Their one idea was to get away from school, they did not really know the parents and were not involved with them. Mind you, there are many good teachers, but some took it on for the money and not much more. The teachers' strikes were very sad. I found teaching a worthwhile life but, in the country, a lonely life. In the country you can't go out and have tea with everybody. You didn't have much social life. But by that time my father was up at Newlands and I used to go home at weekends. I was very lucky in my lodgings which was a good thing.

"I remember one rather funny incident. The managers could be very difficult with their criticisms. The correspondent of the managers came to me one day and said the managers planned to have a meeting and would I attend? They were complaining about the children swearing. I looked at him - remember I was still a very young teacher - and said 'You can have your meeting but I shall say to you that I don't swear. Can any of you honestly say the same?' They cancelled the meeting!

"They used to find fault if the children did anything else outside school. They thought I should be responsible. Lady Mabel Howard was one of our managers. She was very helpful and supportive to me. At one of the meetings she said it must be made clear I wasn't responsible for the behaviour of children out of school. They would complain if Tommy or someone had broken one of their bells or windows. Some parents find it difficult to feel responsible for their children. Some of the managers, like Mr Hodges the vicar, were very good. Others were difficult. Inspectors would come and inspect the school. The Secretary for Education was very pleasant.

"The children would come to school early, at eight o'clock in the morning, and sometimes get into mischief before school started. Before the war and before school meals began, on the odd occasion, I went home for lunch but I took the precaution to lock the school door as I didn't want the children to be up to some mischief during the short time I was away. A farmer wrote an abusive letter to me saying he would report me to the Secretary of Education in Carlise. I told him I would inform him myself and enclosed his letter. The Secretary of Education wrote back saying he approved of my action in locking the school door. This person was the exception. Most people were very pleasant.

"Then there were the hunting days when men hunted the foxes with their dogs on the fells. This was very tempting to the boys who wanted to play truant and go to the hunt. I found the solution because I agreed they should tell me of one day when they could go to the hunt, and that one day was *all* that would be allowed. I don't know if it was the right thing, but it worked and truancy stopped.

"I had good and difficult pupils, but I found out ways of dealing with them. For instance at dinner time they were out of school and they could get into mischief. So I bought them a football. This was a bit expensive for me for a 10/- football didn't last long, but it kept them busy playing! One day they got out of the school at morning break and they were late in returning to class. They returned at twenty past eleven instead of ten past. So I put the clock back ten minutes which meant they had ten minutes less at lunch time. They didn't do that again. I used the stick very seldom for misbehaviour. I felt I should be able to handle pupils without the use of a cane. They knew I wouldn't stand for any nonsense. There was a policeman but he was stationed at Greystoke. He would come to Mungrisdale on certain days, but I didn't need to worry about law and order and the people backed me up.

"I retired in 1953, coronation year, after forty years teaching, and I've been retired thirty-six years. At my retirement I was given a silver teapot which was very nice. I went down to London to be with my sister at the coronation celebrations. I was there for six weeks and then returned to buy a cottage at Bowesdale, about a mile and a half away, and was still friendly with all the parents. I lived in Bowesdale until five years ago when I came here to Abbeyfield in Keswick. I had been ill here in hospital for three months and the doctor said I shouldn't go back. I am quite happy here.

"The school celebrated its centenary soon after I left. Jonathon Scott from Patterdale had left money to build the school. I believe a Mr Turner was the first teacher. Old farmers used to tell me how he would take them round a map of the world pointing out the places with his stick. Somewhere there must be a log book with the names of people connected with the school. It would make interesting reading. I must have been the first woman schoolmistress at Mungrisdale.

"In my retirement I had my gardening, growing fresh vegetables. Since a child I was always interested in wild flowers and of course Mungrisdale gave me scope for learning about and enjoying nature.

The children used to write Bird Tree essays. There was a competition with a shield as a prize and we won it often at Mungrisdale. It was sponsored by the Royal Society for the Protection of Birds who gave the shield. That gave me great pleasure.

"Pupils who did go on after the eleven plus went to Penrith or here to Keswick. I met one in the bank yesterday. She is in her fifties. She said I was looking very well. It's lovely meeting and remembering old pupils. Another who came on to Keswick was William Coulthard who is in agriculture at Wigton. After all these years I have many memories, happy memories of a long life in teaching the 'three R's', religious education, nature study and music.

"To finish these memories, may I just recount a humorous story? The vicar, Mr Hodges, was a young man. He had a car and would drive people some distance to the cinema. It was a car with a dickie behind. One time I was sitting in the back, he turned round - he was driving very fast as he loved to do - and said 'Is the seat comfortable?' I said as I was flung around 'I don't know, I haven't sat on it yet!'

"Mungrisdale was my life, a long and happy one."

EDNA HALL

Mayor and Pet Shop Owner

"Before I was eighteen I was on a trial period of nursing in Birmingham - just about three weeks - when war was declared. I went home for three months but came back to Birmingham and was nursing there for most the war. I went out on continual raids and I would be out all night with ambulances. I can well remember crawling over the rubble with hosepipes everywhere. We had a casualty clearing station with three thousand beds and were operating every night. We used to have practice raids with patients coming in voluntarily to prepare us for the raids. I was a patient myself in those practices. Everything was taken very seriously. I remember one night in particular when we were very short staffed, I was all alone in charge of one ward with eighty patients! Bombs were going off everwhere and fires were all around.

"Later I went into private nursing in Northern Ireland. I nursed Lord Glentoran of Belfast and General Montgomery's mother. She was a fascinating lady, very natural. She lived in a great rambling house. I got her to go to bed for a rest in the afternoons. She always went to bed with a fur coat on, it was a cold house. She would go round and inspect the American troops there. She was so kind, she would take me with her.

"I came to Kendal in 1946. I met my husband at a dance in the Kendal Hotel. I began to help my husband in the yeast business which his grandfather had started. I went round with Matthew in his vans and really got to know the Lake District. We delivered yeast to the hotels and many bakehouses in those days, but very few today. All the bread was made then for there was no wrapped bread like today, no such thing as supermarkets.

"The yeast was made in a yeast factory, just like a distillery. It came from the south, from Liverpool, from Northern Ireland or from Denmark. It usually came by train in those days. It was in seven pound hessian bags. We stored it in the warehouse and made up whatever quantities people might want. I used to stand in the warehouse and help to cut up these little hessian bags and make up ready for delivery.

77

"My husband used to tell me that before the war he used to have carriers to deliver the yeast, not his own vans - but horse and cart in those days.

One of the last carriers to come into the district was an old chap from Sedbergh. He would set off in the morning for Kendal at half past six. He would deliver to the farms as he came into town and arrive in Kendal about eleven o'clock. He'd get his parcels for delivery from Kendal, set off from here back to Sedbergh about half past one and get back about five or six o'clock. He would sleep half the way for his old horse knew where to stop at places as he went along. In the course of time other carriers were getting motorised vehicles. One day somebody said to him 'Why is it you don't get one of these new fangled motor vans? If you set off in the morning at half past eight, you'd be back here at half past one.' He looked at the man and said 'Aye, but what would'e do the other half of the day.'

"My husband's mother had bought a grain and flour shop. People then bought grain for pheasant rearing and for poultry. They took over the business in 1935. They made biscuits for dog food and things like that, for there were no tins of dog food or meats or fish then. Gradually the business developed in the premises we are in now, further down the street.

"We sold yeast at the pet shop too. It was quite hard work in those days with the yeast business and the pet shop. I was in the shop a lot. Today if you go into a pet shop you might see some nuts or grain scattered on the floor which I still try to save, being an old-timer, but in those days if you saw a seed on the floor you picked it up. You couldn't get the seeds or stock you wanted, for remember that was just after the war.

"We began to breed budgerigars and gradually built up and got a few more pets in - for instance rabbits and kittens. We bought the shop next door and made it into one big shop, so we got more animals. We've had alligators, monkeys and snakes. We had a very big tank. We were very careful to observe all the rules. You've got to have a licence to deal in animals, all the small animals like guinea pigs, but for the bigger animals you must have a special licence. We had the young elephant that was on T.V. a lot. We just hired it really for the Kendal Gathering.

"We had a famous macaw called Charlie. It had been on television several times. In those days you queued up for the local cinema. It would walk along the queue and talk to people. It would go up on the telephone wires above the main street and do acrobatics. Everyone knew it. One day we got a phone call from the hospital - 'Charlie's here, what shall we do with him? Will we tie him to the leg of the chair?' We said, 'No, just leave him alone and let him go. He'll find his way back.' And he did. He always did. Sadly one day in the car park we had a lady customer drive over him and kill him. He was accustomed to walk round the car park. She said she saw him but thought he'd get out of the way. We had had him for years and Kendal people were very upset about it.

"We had another parrot called Charlie which used to cry to the manager we had in the shop, 'Come on Mr Williams! Come on Mr Williams!' We had gerbels, Dutch rabbits, long-eared ones, chipmunks, even stick insects. You've a bit of greenery in a tank - very popular with children - and the insect sticks to the stick, almost seems a part of it. Children have got to peer closely to see them and feed them. We've all types of tropical and cold water fish. We supply people who have tanks at home.

"It's important a pet shop is up to standard, or you wouldn't be granted a licence. You must know about the care of animals. For instance we don't want people to come in and buy a dog on the spur of the moment. The staff is trained that whoever comes in to buy an animal, they've got to size up the customer and judge if he or she is really interested. Supposing, just supposing someone's having a drink and maybe not acting as reasonably as he might, and he comes in and wants to buy a pet as a Christmas present on the spur of the moment and then later gets tired of it. So we are very strict who we sell pets to. We don't sell a pet to a youngster unless we know he has got written permission from his parent. Our daughter, who is qualified with distinction in pet management - she was one of the first to pass the exam a few years ago - is very particular about all these matters. In the Pet Store of the Year competition she was first runner-up in that. She knows more now about pet management than I or her father do for she's young and up-to-date. The big thing is that she's very fond of animals and interested in them. That's how all pet shop owners should be.

"My husband and I were interested in the Lakes Gliding Club. We were founder members and I became its first secretary. A friend said to me, would I stand for the Council? I had no intention of doing anything like that. I had joined the Professional and Business Women's Club and was only in it for three months when they asked me to become secretary. I went on to be president and then international chairman. During this time I had got used to a bit of public speaking and got a bit more confidence. I was made the President of the Chamber of Trade. I had been a councillor for a number of years. Matthew and I had canvassed in the Castle Ward. I stood as a strictly independent person. In those days I didn't think politics should enter into it, it was the town that mattered. I can say I worked hard because I believe if I'm going to do something, I must do it properly if I can. Anyway I was elected with quite a handsome majority.

"I went away for a week's tuition down south. That helped me a bit. There were twenty-four councillors and six aldermen. What interested me, after a number of years, was that there were fewer than half the council members who were Kendalians. After about a dozen years in the Council I was asked to be mayor. I had been vice-chairman of the Housing Committee which was a big committee. I was the chairman of the Museum Committee. After the reorganisation of local government I was on most of the committees. I was on both Kendal Council and South Lakeland District Council. The Town Council met in the evenings and the South Lakeland District Council had meetings during the day, so that helped. I'd be involved with the Gas and Electricity Councils which meant travelling to London or to Carlisle. I was made Mayor of Kendal in 1976.

"I enjoyed my years as Mayor of Kendal. I had never realised how many ordinary people did so much voluntary good work and never mentioned it. There are so many good people around and one doesn't hear of them. I met so many doing really hard work, helping others, and it was never mentioned! Being mayor gave you the privilege of meeting folk like these.

"During the year Prince Charles came up to Sizergh Castle and to Windermere, I met him at the Yacht Club on Windermere. I think he's one of the tops. He's so natural. He seems to consider everybody and everything - a very natural, charming young man. We're lucky to have him as a future king. I remember when we were in the launch side by side, they gave him a mug of tea. He looked at me and said 'Haven't you got a cup yet? Where's your tea? I said 'Oh, it'll be coming.' He meant that. He wasn't being funny. His concern was for me. Later we saw him coming into Windermere in this beautiful car, for he had been up Kirkstone way. He came to me and said 'Are you going to Sizergh Castle tonight?' We had been talking about my Mayor's chain and that sort of thing. He said 'I'll see you there then.' And he asked me 'Is it far?' He looked tired; the air up here, if you're not used to it, makes you feel sleepy. I said 'Just about ten or eleven miles?' He said 'That's good. So I'll see you then.' Later at Sizergh he came along and talked to me and the others. He remembered all of us. He made a wonderful natural speech that night.

"It caused a bit of a sensation when I got Matthew officially recognised as mayoress. It sounds funny but you'll understand it better if I explain what was really behind it. Normally if there was a lady mayor her husband, on occasions, would accompany her. If you are officially recognised as mayoress, the attendant on duty must do what he is told by both mayor and mayoress. It was expected my daughter would be mayoress, but Matthew and I had always worked closely together and he had been such a support to me that I wanted us to be officially recognised together. The Council did recognise this and it was passed.

"Several councils in the south wrote to us where they were in the same position, but we were the first. Only last week there were people up; Winchester was one of the place the husband became mayoress. It meant when I was going to a function I could have my husband there, supporting, as mayoress. I never wanted him to have the title for its own sake. It was for my benefit in my official duties to the community.

"My long experience has taught me many things. First of all I'd say, listen to ordinary people and think about what they say, take note of what they say. Be a good listener. I remember the day when I wouldn't have spoken in public, for anybody! I know it sounds rude, but an old lady of eighty-four, when I was President of the Business and Professional Women's Club, said to me - for I was young and green then and thought I could never do public speaking, and although I had done one or two votes of thanks, when I stood up my knees would shake - she said 'Now stop it. Everybody has to go through this. Just remember when you're speaking, look above the heads of your audience and think how they all sit on the toilet just the same as you do! Forget about them and just be natural.' It may sound rude but I've always remembered that.

"Another thing my experiences have taught me is to try to be considerate of other people's feelings. It helps them often just by listening to them, to their views or to their distress or by whatever little bit of encouragement you can give them. The majority of folk are so kind. We were surprised particularly at the number of youngsters who would do a lot of good work, helping in hospitals, helping old people to do their shopping, all on their own initiative. If some young person does something wrong it's headlines. There's not so much about the good that's done."

BOB CLEASBY

Making Shoes (1)

"I began in K Shoes in 1929 when I was put on to junior jobs like putting lasts away, and working with an old prehistoric machine which breasted. In fact some of the jobs I did are now done away with. I went into the Finishing Department and it was there I met up with Jim Major. By that time I was married and on incentive working. If you had £5 in your wages, you were well-paid before the war.

"The firm of K Shoes in Kendal was started by the Somervell brothers in 1842. They had a tannery, tanning bottom leather - heavier skins for the bottom leather of shoes. The tanning pits are still there, underground, but you can't see them now - underneath the car park in the North Yard, just next to Netherfield bridge. The Somervells had a big house in Stramongate. The family firm didn't go public till the fifties, a private firm for over a hundred years. They started with tanning and then broke out into manufacturing.

"They got to the stage where they were buying leather and giving the jobs out to houses in Kendal. Then they found out people were putting cheaper bottom leather on and selling their more expensive leather. To get round that they produced the well-known K design which they branded into the leather. That's how the copyright came. It's interesting that this is the only single letter allowed to be used in registration.

"The people used to finish the shoes off in their houses and bring them t'shop, as they'd say. Often you wouldn't see them for three or four days for they'd go on the booze with the money. In those days they were a hard-drinking people.

"Then when the railway was built here there were buildings put up to house the Irish labourers who worked on it. After they left the Somervells had them for their first factory. These buildings are gone now. When I started with K Shoes in 1929 that was the only factory there was, except one at Lancaster where they only made uppers - stitching them together. They were cut in Kendal, sent to Lancaster for stitching, then back to Kendal to be finished. They still have the Lancaster factory, making men 's uppers but not ladies'.

82

"Some expansion of K Shoes was to Askam in the fifties, near Barrow-in-Furness. It was a godsend to the Askam village. The first building they had was York House, a big hall in those days, but it was in the early sixties their first factory opened there. Again in the early fifties they established the men's shoe factory at Low Mills, just down the road from here. They had already moved the sole department down there, first to Low Mills which was then just a big house. Then they built the factory down there. Later we expanded to Workington too, and Millom in Cumberland. Millom had been a real black spot for unemployment and some Millom people had been working at Askam, so when they opened at Millom the folk there didn't need to travel.

"Just after the war we did the whole manufacturing process in our factory. Then the men's shoes went to the Low Mill and the ladies' were at the Old Netherfield, as we called it. A lot of people think there is a place of that name but there isn't. It's Netherfield Works. There actually was a field there, at the bottom end of the original factory, which was termed the Netherfield. You got the Netherfield Football Club and the Netherfield Cricket Club. At that time the firm was employing perhaps about twenty-two hundred at its best. From the late seventies to the early eighties we had a bad spell and there were redundancies.

"One interesting move was when K Shoes bought two existing factories in Norwich in the sixties. They had been owned by W.H.H. Clark - not C. & J. Clark who took us over later - they were lovely factories and they were both producing ladies' court shoes of good quality. People down in Norwich were noted for high quality. A good bit before this we had bought the rights to manufacture American Red Cross shoes and we changed the name to Gold Cross, manufactured on their lasts. I think it was 1/3d we paid in the old money in royalties on each pair. We had a department for Gold Cross and we did well in that. All the best operatives were put into the Gold Cross Department.

"Relationships on the shop floor were quite good until the early thirties. I remember we had a strike in the Finishing Department in 1934. This began when suede shoes came through on racks and there was a pair of gloves on each rack which you had to wear. One day the director came down and caught one of the operatives not wearing the gloves and he suspended him for a fortnight; the men wouldn't have it and thought it was unjust. They had meetings and decided to have a 'sit-in,' as we call it today. They were told 'You don't work, you just stay by your machines.'

"The management posted notices saying if no one wanted to work, they needn't come back, but they took no notice and came back to work. A telegram came from the trade-union advising them to resume work pending the arrival of a union representative. Well, you know what they said - 'Pooh!' The next thing was, in came a police sergeant with six or seven constables along with the director and each individual was asked if he would work. If the answer was 'No,' the police said 'Get out.' There was no rough stuff. Everybody just walked out except two people. One was a foreman's son and the other a chap who had spent many years in Canada and America and had come back again. After that they went round and sacked about thirty people, including one woman, for being hot-heads. They wrote to employers in the town telling them not to employ these people for they were hot-heads! It took a long time for relationships to improve.

"The war came and I often wondered what would have happened to some of us if the war hadn't happened. In the works I was on the shop floor and also I was in the St. John's Ambulance, so immediately war broke out we were away; we were like territorials. When I came back at the end of 1945 I realised it was no good to me. You seemed to be back on a different level. I had done quite well as a warrant officer in the Medics and now you wanted something else. I left the shop floor in 1948 to go on the export side, which didn't in fact materialise. For that purpose they wanted me to go into our Costing Department, to train for costings. I was costing the men's range of shoes and costing the export. The idea was for me to move on, but when it came to the point when they wanted me to make my next move the head of the Costing Department said 'No way, I need him,' so I stayed in Costing. Then, right out of the blue, the wages manager was sacked and I was sitting in his chair the following morning. From there we paid all the wages. While I had been in Costing I had started negotiations with the trade-union. Then they decided they would split up wages and each office would pay its own wages, but this time I.R. had come into being and I went full-time on to industrial relations. We hadn't such a thing as a Personnel Department at that time. Then the firm took in a personnel manager and I worked with him, and from that grew the whole Personnel Department. He is now personnel director. Under his wing my friend Jim Major came into that and Jim and I were together again, for we had both started on the shop floor in the Finishing Department before the war. We sometimes wonder if we'd have been satisified with our lot if it hadn't been for the war.

"There are those who'll tell you in the industry there's only one trade - they're the clickers who cut out the upper material when it was all done by hand. Now it's all done by presses. It was a craft held in the very highest esteem. The clicker went to work with a bowler hat, collar and tie. With a knife he cut round the pattern. It was so skilled in those days for they were working with all genuine leathers. Today there are leathers too, but they're processed and the flaws aren't obvious. It was an art working with the quality leathers. In so much of the leathers nowadays what happens is the tanneries can hide a multitude of sins. Polyurethane finishes are used on top of leathers. So gradually the old skills are eaten away.

"They started manufacturing mock crocodile leathers, known as mock croc, with an embossed finish. The clickers at the time were up in arms. I was involved in trying to get incentive work for all this, getting prices for working with the mock crocodile. Finally they sent up to Kendal one of the leading lights of the trade-union and the chap that came up was a man called Jones, probably in his late fifties, who had been a clicker himself. We got nowhere and, finally, after another meeting he just looked at them and said 'Come on lads, this is definitely a fair offer. I've been a clicker myself and I've cut genuine crocodile shoes. You've had a fair price.' Needless to say they never asked Jones to come up again. You see, we got together and talked about things. In those days there were no industrial relations, or rather, the industrial relations was me. Nowadays in industrial relations you're damn near to becoming a lawyer! I was doing this and another part of the job was looking after the wages. The clickers, for the incentive work, used to have a pricing committee and they'd have their meeting with management. They'd ask for another ha'penny, then another and finally settle a price and that's how prices were fixed. They were the top earners.

"I remember when the second lot of presses came in, the clickers refused to take any kind of reduction whatever. That was where the big slip-up came, when we didn't press too hard. There was a scheme for leather saving but the clickers simply wouldn't have it. It ran for twelve months before they finally accepted it, with meeting after meeting! What they really had thrown away was £5 a week. With the other departments piece-pricing was a matter of trial and error. Piece-pricing was very difficult. After the war, time-study came in. There is some piece work left but all the rest is time-study. But to my mind operatives can fool the time-study man. You've got to be a really good time-study man not to be fooled. A lot depends on the co-operation of the supervisor and his knowledge. If he knows his job and there's good liaison with the engineer, he'll get it right.

"K Shoes have always stood for high standard, but every manufacturing firm needs the challenge of keeping up standards. For instance we manufacture shoes for Marks & Spencer. They are very strict. I know, for my son-in-law deals with them. As a matter of fact one of the reasons why we started doing business with Marks & Spencer was because they were so ruthless for quality. Put it this way. We have all our own shop outlets, and a lot of independent shops as well, several thousand independents and, say, four hundred of our own shops. With the best will in the world, those people with possible complaints, and sending some footwear back, does not stimulate you to a high enough level to be really ruthless with yourself. You need someone outside your own set-up to be ruthless with you, kicking your backside. Now Marks & Spencer do that, which is good for everybody. They have their own specifications and their own skilled men who do the inspections, and if you have anything below the two per cent level they don't want it. It's good for you and for working to the highest quality of manufacturing.

"One of my memories was the visit of the Duke of York and Elizabeth, later King George and his Queen, to the factory before the war. That was a great day. They painted a white line right round the factory, the route they were going to take. That was the first time the supervisors wore white. They were all issued with a white overall. Photographs were taken and off they went to Oxenholme. Each operative could choose one and the photographs were framed and presented by the firm.

"In my retirement I'm always busy. I was a sick visitor for K's employees and do the rounds of the hospital, and I'm on the Council of the British Legion. I've many memories of days in K's."

JIM MAJOR

Making Shoes (2)

"I started working in K Shoes in Kendal in 1937. I was doing the kinds of jobs lads were given. But with the war in the offing they started teaching lads like me skilled jobs, and by the time the war came along I was doing skilled shoe-making jobs in the Finishing Department, like trimming. But unbeknown to my foreman I had volunteered for the Navy. So I was away from shoe-making for five years, but returned to it when the war was over.

"I've seen many changes in the ways shoes are made since joining the firm in 1937. We have a repair factory which still does a lot of the old processes, almost the last of the breed; processes like the old welting process where the sole is stitched on. There's a couple of lads up there who can still do it the hard way, but over the years there's been a slow process of change. The first change was probably the introduction of the argo process, a cement solution. That came in the twenties. The big changes came after the war.

"Before the war we were using cement to stick on soles. From the fifties the changes came with the use of new cements, first the neoprene cements, then the polyurethane cements. These were appoxyresin types. With the polyurethane came solid rod cement that could be fed through a machine and spewed onto the right position on the shoe. It was heated inside the machine and directed onto the position on the shoe where you wanted to stick it. Hot plates came across and held the shoe in position. The whole thing was held for a second or two while it set hard. That really revolutionised the whole business.

"The new cements meant we could now concentrate on making shoes with machines that could mechanically do a lot more of the old handwork, do away with the nails and tacks and so on. We could now make the shoe more flexible as well and lighter. Then plastics provided the plastic heel and cut out more operations. Plastics were used in shoe components generally and we were able to make bottom materials out of synthetics. Of course plastics had been used before the war in bottom materials such as uskides and crepe, but these were heavy and ugly. Now modern plastics are used to make light ladies' soles with more wearing power than before. More recently we had the big power-injection moulding machine using the polyurethanes which now produce injection moulds, very hard-wearing. These shoes I've got on now I've been wearing constantly for two years. This injection moulding does away with whole departments. There's no finishing required.

"Another change is the buying in of components. You look at a shoe now, the sole and the heel are not leather, they're synthetic materials bought in. I used to be in the Finishing Department. Great hand skill was needed there. I think there's hardly anyone who can make a pair of shoes now from start to finish.

"When war broke out I was in the Finishing Department at Netherfield. During the war I served with the Royal Navy as a leading signalman in the destroyer *H.M.S. Wrestler*. I was on the Russian convoys, the Atlantic convoys, the D-day landings and the Sicily landings. In the Far East I was in the Ramree Island landing and the Rangoon landing. After the war I married Helen Wood from the Closing Room at K Shoes. By the time the first copy of the K Shoes company magazine was published in October 1949, we had a little boy, Peter. Actually my photograph was on the front cover of that first copy.

"When I came back from the war I said 'Find me something, I'm fed up hanging around,' so they said 'Just go the stores' and I said 'That'll do.' In those days there were just the head storeman and myself. As the firm began to grow, the company realised they needed supervisors and had to train people up to run different departments. That would be in 1949. They invited applications and I applied for a job which I got in Assembly. This was collecting all the finished components, putting them in job lots and feeding them out to the manufacturing units. This was 1951. Then as the whole company grew that department grew, and I got to be manager. After that I became assistant to the superintendent looking after the whole of the manufacturing and then I became factory superintendent. It was now the early seventies. At that time the last of the Somervells - the founder family of the firm - left; he had been in Administration and I was asked if I'd go into that and I more or less continued the rest of my time there. Administration involved the Finance and Personnel departments so I linked up here with my friend Bob Cleasby with whom I started on the shop floor many years ago.

"Five years earlier C. & J. Clark had taken over the company. It was during a bad period for the company when our shares were low.

Ward White - it was a chap named McWatters - made a daylight raid and bought fifteen per cent of the shares with the supposed intention of buying us out, but *I* think he was just after a quick return. We were at panic stations. It was then we approached C. & J. Clark to see if they were interested. Clarks were always very friendly, indeed I used to go down to Clarks in the old days to look at their processes. They always said they would never put themselves on the stock exchange, but they said to us 'Well, just carry on and if you get into real trouble we'll come to your help.' They had already bought an enormous number of our shares over the years. Then when they heard we were in bad straits and would possibly be taken over, they arranged a meeting and within the matter of a week it was all settled.

"It had been a bad time. When you have someone making a bid like Ward White, all sorts of things come out of the woodwork. We had a lot of key shop sites. Now those alone, if anybody got their hands on them, could be sold off. Also on the manufacturing side so much cheap footwear was being imported. What happened now was, if a particular style or construction of shoe was being developed in the market, we would look at it. If we thought we'd have a use for it, at this stage we'd get it made outside, for if it didn't go well and we'd set up a department to manufacture it, we'd have had to close it down. So that's why we used outside firms, doing a development job by contracting out. These are special little firms who do nothing but MTO, made to order. They haven't got a brand name of their own; they make to your specification and you go along and inspect it, just as Marks & Spencer inspect the quality of the shoes we make for them.

"We have whole teams of designers designing K Shoes; separate designing departments concentrating on men's, women's and children's footwear. Shoes are wear-tested. If a person is the right size and does a lot of walking, the firm says 'Take these and wear them constantly and we'll check them, see what they're like after a ten mile test.' At the end of the day the person gets the shoes. We do it with people like nurses who have a lot of walking to do. Kiddies are wear-tested too.

"I retired from the firm in 1986 after nearly fifty years in the footwear industry. Nowadays K Shoes must have about fifteen hundred working for them. Then there are the people who work in the shops and they have about three hundred shops, so that means another thousand. So overall it's a big workforce.

"As far as the buildings are concerned, the original Netherfield factory isn't used for production at all now. The headquarters building next to Netherbridge is purely administrative. The other factories in Kendal are Low Mills down the river - it's for men's shoes - and the Springer factory for men's Springer sandals, casual shoes. There's the Millbank factory and Kentside factory. The whole production area stretches from Netherfield right down the side of the river. Still in the Kendal area K shoes hire a big warehouse at Meal Bank for leather and components.

"In Cumbria, outside Kendal, there's the production factory at Barrow-in-Furness for women's and children's shoes; another at Millom for children's shoes and a unit at Shap where they make uppers for shoes, stitching pieces of leather together. The reason for this decentralising is that the shoe industry is very labour intensive, so you have to take the work to the workforce.

"In west Cumbria there's a lot of female labour which is good for shoe-making. It counterbalances the heavy industries which are in decline and also there were grants to go there. Then there's a big closing unit in Lancaster and also in Norwich which K Shoes took over in the 1960's from W.H.H. Clark. Now of course K Shoes are owned by another Clark, nothing to do with W.H.H. Clark.

"Technology has made a tremendous difference to K Shoes. They now sell about five and a half million shoes a year. In 1976 there was almost double the present workforce which made about the same number of shoes. So they make out the same amount with just over half that workforce. The industry is slowly being automated. So technology, although shoe-making is a craft industry, has had a great effect.

"Fashions change when you think back to the sixties with winkle-pickers, then platform shoes. These tend to be youth cults and get absorbed into the mainstream of fashion, but it seems that the days of these big trends are practically gone. Nowadays you might get a temporary fashion which may have been started by a T.V. series or a film or a pop group. The styling of shoes at the present time is much more conservative. The designers in K's have their different interests, men's women's and children's. Many of them have degrees in shoe-designing. K's shoes aren't what you might call leaders in show fashion, they are one step back from fashion. It's good styling rather than fashion shoes.

"K Shoes, the only single letter brand to be registered, is famous. I enjoyed working in it. It has been interesting to see the changes in a fine craft industry over many years."

OLIVE CLARKE M.B.E.

Voluntary Service

"My father was a farmer and I was born about four miles from where I live now at Crooklands, having lived in just two houses all my life. I went to the local Old Hutton Primary School, which had a big influence on my life. It was a husband and wife set-up, as schools often were in those days, a Mr and Mrs Syddall. Mr Syddall had a wide vision and he was a great musician. He had been in India as a soldier. There was a map on the wall and there it was, the Empire, all coloured red. We then had a sort of national pride with the Union Jack flying on Empire day. I know today we are told not to be nationalistic, but I believe the right kind of pride in our country is needed very badly.

"In those days, when there wasn't the same chance of knowing what was going on outside our part of the countryside, Mr Syddall encouraged a knowledge of the wider world and he gave us an interest in it. Mrs Syddall made us work very hard and that did us no harm. In time I got a scholarship to Kendal High School.

"There was a club at Hutton already established called the Young Farmers' Club. I joined this and I also joined the W.I.. This would be 1938. I was still at school. The Young Farmers' Club has been a wonderful educational movement for the countryside. There are many people today who give public service to the community in Cumbria and they were in the beginning encouraged by the Young Farmers' Club. They include magistrates, county councillors, people prominent in the National Farmers' Union and in all walks of public life. The Young Farmers' Club also contribute to what was then an industry that couldn't express itself. It encouraged public speaking. The first Young Farmers' public speaking contest in the area was in 1938. I happened to win it and there's the certificate on the wall to prove it. I was the first female county chairman of the Young Farmers' Club and the first woman president.

"We were brought up in the tradition that you did what you could in the countryside and there was always voluntary service for the church, for the school and the idea of 'help your neighbour.' There was nothing new about it. It was a very amateur voluntary service but it was always there.

"I became a magistrate in 1960. There were a great number of motoring cases following bad accidents on Shap Fell. It was the main artery north. All the lorry drivers went up Shap which was notorious. Since the M6 was made there aren't so many accidents as there were then.

"I was a member of the Juvenile Panel for a great many years. Of course everybody who is a magistrate is not on the Juvenile Panel. Juvenile court magistrates are chosen from people who are expected to be really involved and interested in the wellbeing of our young folk, especially between the ages of ten and seventeen. Unfortunately fifty-five per cent of all the house burglaries in this country are done by juveniles under the age of seventeen. There have been changes during my time in the Juvenile Court. The 1961 Children and Young Peoples' Act said children were in need of care and not of punishment. I've always felt caring should be a priority in the minds of magistrates in as much as, through whatever appropriate punishment meted out, young people might think again. There are many elements that are needed in the work, such as plain common sense, a real sense of locality and of a person's background. All are needed but a common sense approach is, I think, the first requisite in dealing with youngsters. I was very happy to be chairman of that court for so many years.

"In those days there was no obligation for a magistrate to take training. There was the odd course at Manchester University and I went to that voluntarily. Nowadays prospective magistrates take a formal course of training. I think in the end the best training is experience.

"This is how I came to be a magistrate. At that time it so happened that magistrates Mr and Mrs Pennington were spending part of the winter in South Africa - they were famous Westmorland names - also Mrs Crewdson was ill. The point was in those days we had to sit as seven magistrates in the court. Now of course we sit as three, a deputy chairman with a magistrate on either side. Anyway I was asked to make up the number that was needed then, if you like I was the very lowest. That's where and when I began. My years there have been very happy.

"My years with the W.I. have also been happy ones. It is a wonderful national asset. It's motto is 'For Home and Country', its object is to develop and improve conditions around us. It used to be primarily involved with the countryside, but it's now recognised that many women of countryside origins live in towns and so it embraces a membership in both country and town. It's been going since about 1915 and it has done so much for the countryside, so much for the individual, for the wider education and opportunities of women which many would never have dreamed of in years past! I have heard the Queen Mother at the annual gathering in the Albert Hall describe the W.I. as the guardian of the countryside. It has proved an influence on our national life because through our resolutions no government of any colour dare ignore the united clamour of half a million women. In an effort like 'Keep Britain Tidy' the W.I. has participated for many years. It hasn't just kept abreast of events, it has often been ahead of the times on practical issues.

"I was in touch with the W.I. from about the age of fourteen because of my mother. As time went on I became more involved with its growing opportunities for service in the community. Government departments would ask for W.I. members to be appointed to national committees. They would approach national headquarters and ask for people of experience to be nominated. That's why in 1968 I came to be on a national committee. I was nominated by Cumberland and Westmorland for membership of the Transport Users' Consultative Committee for the Department of Trade and the Department of Transport acting jointly, and in 1979 I was invited by the minister to be chairman. Just before the Conservative government came to power in 1979 I was given the M.B.E. because, as the press said at the time, I had given a lifetime of service to the country. But the country had given so much to me as an ordinary person through these wonderful bodies like the Young Farmers' and the W.I. As I said, they are wonderful organisations.

"Some issues rouse strong feelings. One was the threatened closure of the Settle-Carlisle railway line. I was made chairman of the public hearing about this problem. Our recommendation to the minister was that the line should remain open. The report weighed three and a half stones in paper. For hours we listened to the arguments, from groups like the County Council - to ordinary individuals. I believe individuals matter. We had great sympathy for the individual. I remember listening to a high power County Council dissertation with all the figures and statistics worked out. Then there followed a little man who said 'I object because of my queens, and they're all virgin queens.' I felt my mouth dropping and my eyes almost popped out. I looked round the crowded hall wondering what was coming next, but in fact he was talking about his bees and how he wanted to take his bees on the train and take them to the heather. He legitimately objected on the ground of hardship. Now the point is the law says we must assess on the grounds of hardship, among other things, and his case was based on personal hardship. While others would be denied the pleasure of the scenery if the line were closed, was this strictly hardship? These things had to be carefully thought out.

"As a farmer's daughter and a farmer's wife, I love the country. I love this county, Cumbria, it's where so many of my interests are focused. The W.I. with its interests in countryside development has been a great motivation in all my activities, and as a farmer's wife I've always been interested in land. I was the first woman chairman of the County Landowners Association for Westmorland and Furness. In a way my interest in the C.L.A. was similar to my interest in the W.I. The C.L.A. deals with land ownership and land occupiers. I believe we're only caretakers of the land we own. There is a great deal of misunderstanding about C.L.A., seventy-five per cent of the members own less than a hundred acres of land. It's a mistaken view that it's only the owners of huge estates, indeed a great many members own less than two acres. There's a real cross-section, a real mix of the kinds of owners, and I believe that's as it should be. It's truly democratic. In this respect it's like the W.I.. I'm now the Cumbrian President of the Westmorland and Furness branch. I have served five years on the National Legal and Parliamentary Committee in London. I've seen that, just as the W.I. has had influence at national level on government departments, so the C.L.A. had had through its national committees. The concept is care-taking of the countryside. That's my main interest.

"Regarding the W.I., a lot of people may laugh about us singing *Jerusalem*, my daughters have joked and said to me 'What about the arrows of desire, Mother?' Now, I'm a parish councillor and the Parish Council's made up of ordinary people who have been caring for many years for this green and pleasant land. I've been a school governor and have been involved with the important Cumbria College of Agriculture and Forestry which has encouraged agricultural interests in the county. The English Tourist Board invited me to judge the competition they run which is called 'Britain in Bloom', and which is really improvements in the environment generally, from the tourist angle.

"If I had the time I would spend a lot of time gardening, for I love it. Over the years Arthur and I have put a lot of work into the garden

94

and land here at Kaker Mill Farm. My husband has always believed you don't need to go in for grandiose schemes to develop the countryside. We love to see animal life around us. We have the guinea fowls, the geese on the beck and Albert and Victoria, our husband and wife peacocks.. We've always had cats. At present I've Big Boy and Little Man, ginger toms, and we have the ponies. Arthur has been Father Christmas using the white pony and trap.

"I'm a great believer in country life and everybody can make their contribution. It isn't everybody that's going to take the chair and it's often the chairman or chairwoman who puts the chairs away! We've all got some contribution to make.

"I've had a life of great interest and variety, but there are certain bed-rock things that are really important. First I think there was the day I married. Marriage to me is important. I'm grateful to my husband and my daughters. I'm also grateful to the fact I was brought up to a very simple Christian faith. I'm not interested in deep theological thinking, but the Church matters a great deal to me. I remember once I was asked to speak at a service in the lovely church at Howgill at a lambing thanksgiving. It's in a valley hemmed in by the fells where I'd been many times to the W.I. Because they don't have harvests they display their common sense by having a lambing thanksgiving instead of a harvest thanksgiving. It was a happy experience with the lambs all around us. My faith is a simple one and I think my motto is 'Let me not be so heavenly minded that I am no earthly good.' In the early days on my father's farm when times were bad, I was taught to count my blessings and told to keep my eyes on the stars but my feet on the ground. I'm grateful for the opportunities life has given me."

JOHN WATTON

Border Territorial and Artist

"My father was a soldier fighting in France during the First World War. When I was a baby - I was born in 1915 - my mother took me, as some of the mothers were allowed to take their babies, across to France. There was a Roman Catholic community of mothers set up at Bayeux and I was one of the war babies in this convent. Fathers who were on short leave from the front came to see their wives and children and my father saw me through a grille, for of course he wasn't allowed in the convent, but mothers were allowed out.

"I stayed a couple of years and left France after the big victory parade in July 1919. I watched that in the Champs Elysée in Paris. Then I came back to England. The women who had stayed in the convent became Roman Catholics and so did I. I came up to Kendal and got a job in K Shoes thanks to a friend of my father. I just went through the factory doing different jobs in departments like the soling room and finally went into the advertising side and stayed there.

"In the early days as an apprentice I earned about ten bob a week. But I joined the Territorial Army and through that made quite a bit of money. K Shoes were very good, they allowed me a fortnight's holiday on full pay. Then I was allowed to go to Territorial Camp where I got full pay plus a bonus given for loss of pay which, of course, I had never lost. Later I was given another fortnight's holiday to go on a course to Sandhurst or Catterick or other bases. All this was on full pay from K's and army pay as well, so I made quite a reasonable amount. I supplemented this by long-distance professional running.

"When I joined the Territorial Army I moved into lodgings in Kendal where I shared with a number of grammar-school masters. I paid thirty bob a week for full board and lodgings. There were probably four or five to a room. Then the war came and the most adventurous part of my life began.

"I was in command of a mortar platoon in the Fourth Battalion in the Border Regiment. We were helping to cover the big retreat at the time of Dunkirk. Sir John Burgess was Company Commander. I was a lieutenant at that time. We had been left behind to guard the rear-

Above: Olive Clark, first woman president of the County Show. *(Chapter 14. Voluntary Service)*

Left: Olive was the first woman president of the Young Farmers' Club. Here she is seen at a celebration of the Golden Jubilee of Hutton Young Farmers.

John Watton. *(Chapter 15. Border Territorial and Artist)*
Below: A rare photograph of Colditz, where John's talent as an artist helped
Dutch prisoners to escape.

Right:
Joe Bradbury.
(Chapter 16. Making Paper)

Joe was in the Border
Regiment during the
1939-45 war.

Below:
Percy Duff MBE., with
Mayor Hadley examining a
trowel and gavel used in
the extension to the Town
Hall in 1893. They were
returned from America.
*(Chapter 17. Town
Treasurer)*

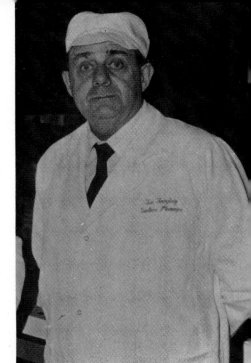

Right:
Joe Faughey
(Chapter 18. Making Biscuits in Carlisle)

Above: An early graceful example of protective clothing at Carrs of Carlisle

Above: Gathering coal from the beach (c.1920).
Right: James Blaney.
(Chapter 20. Coal Miner)

Left:
Geoff Gawith, examining leaves in the factory.
(Chapter 19. Snuff & Tobacco Manufacturer)

Left: Jim Noble MBE. Jim became sub-editor of the Westmorland Gazette.
(Chapter 21. Journalist)

Below: Edward McIntyre.
(Chapter 22. Shipbuilding at Barrow-in-Furness

Below: Launch of HM Submarine 'Orpheus' by Mrs Taylor on 17th Nov. 1959.

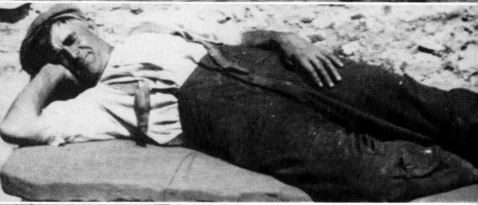

Top: Arthur Pickthall. *(Chapter 23. Ninety-seven Years of Farming)*
Above: Resting after haymaking.

Left:
Bill Guest.
(Chapter 24. Sellafield and Nuclear Power)

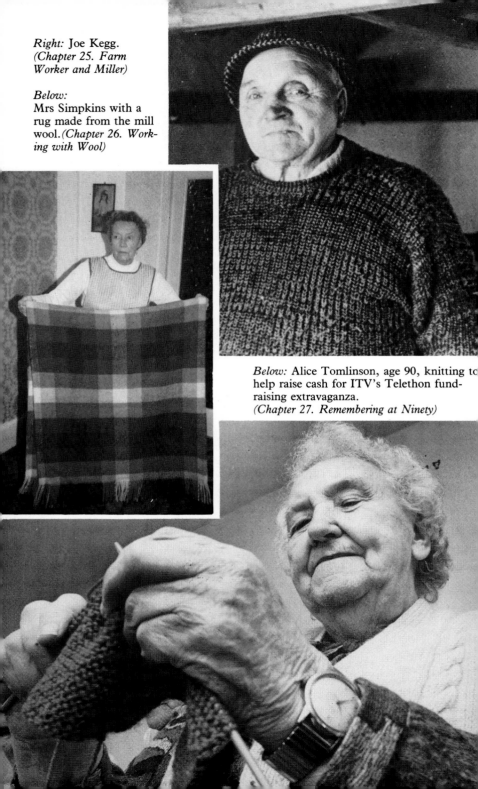

Right: Joe Kegg.
(Chapter 25. Farm Worker and Miller)

Below:
Mrs Simpkins with a rug made from the mill wool. *(Chapter 26. Working with Wool)*

Below: Alice Tomlinson, age 90, knitting to help raise cash for ITV's Telethon fund-raising extravaganza.
(Chapter 27. Remembering at Ninety)

guard. At Dunkirk they wanted to get back all the best troops they possibly could, the guards and regular troops. We were a line of communication troops doing petrol dumps, ammunition dumps and so on. We were asked to hold the rear, to hold up as much as possible the enemy advance by preventing the Germans using certain roads.

"I was with 'D' Company, the Kendal Company, in Incheville. It was there we were all captured, just a small village you couldn't see on the map. 'D' Company was in the Town of Missing Men Company, so-called because we were all taken.

"It happened like this, for it might be interesting to Kendal folk. We went in on June 7th. I was ordered to give overhead fire with mortars, over the heads of our own men. As I didn't want to drop anything on our own troops, I decided to go into the village where our troops were, rather than run the danger of bombing our own men. I could never have shown up in Kendal again if that had happened! I was greeted by Colonel Hopkinson and we fired our mortars at the Germans. Colonel Hopkinson was shot in the eye and the Second-in-Command had been killed. It was our own Bryan Stilling of K Shoes who came up and reported the Second-in-Command had been killed. There was Chris Deighton who inherited 'D' Company, Sub-Lieutenant Crossley and also Second Lieutenant Williams in charge of Transport had the Bren carriers. We had a conference and decided to hold the village to the end.

"We held five houses and then the Germans began to come through. Later Eric Linklater, the Scottish author, described us as "a nest of wrathful Englishmen." The first Germans, motor-cycle dispatch riders, began to arrive - very brave men indeed. The first one we killed, struck by an anti-tank rifle, and he lay by the side of the road. We learned later he was only nineteen years old. Then we got another dispatch rider and there followed the first of the German staff cars.

"Remember the background of our men. They were Cumbrians and had a feel for a situation like this - descendants of moss troopers and Border rievers. We fired with anti-tank rifles and the two German officers were killed. There was a pause, then another staff car entered the village. When we fired the two occupants managed to get out and they ran up the road, climbed up to a hedge, fell back down the slope, but scrambled up again, and they got away. Williams ran up to the car and smashed the opaque windscreen, jumped into the car, drove it and smashed into the back of the first car. He jumped out and shouted back to us 'Loot it, you fools, loot it!' We crawled out and ran to the car and dragged out of the boot chocolates and cigars. We got back and handed them round. 'Would you care for a cigar?' 'Don't mind if I do.' Typical Cumbrian in a situation like this!

"Then a third staff car suddenly appeared with four in it. It hit a road block and overturned. Three were killed outright but the fourth was the German driver. He shouted 'Wounded, wounded.' We dragged him out and wrapped him up in a blanket.

"Altogether we hadn't quite fifty of us. There had been some Sherwood Foresters but they were withdrawn, they had had very bad casualties. One of our men, a butcher, killed a cow and we had that to eat.

"Soon a German Air Force staff car appeared. The two men in it were both killed. From it we got medical supplies which proved very useful. We were short of medical people, just two stretcher bearers and a French doctor in the village. A man's leg had been cut off and another man's arm, but they both died. The French doctor was a deserter from the French Army and he made good use of the medical supplies when we were under fire. I remember this doctor bending over the wounded and squeezing all the pus out of gangrenous wounds. He did a marvellous job. the conditions were terrible. All the lavatories were full and we had one man to keep them clean.

"The next staff car nosing into the village was a naval officer and his driver. The driver was terribly wounded and we got the officer alive. A couple of German lorries came in and the drivers were forced out into the road. One young German ran down the road and I got him to carry German wounded to the hospital. Then we had a meal. Stanley Gudgeon, under fire, had dug up potatoes and we had the cow. Williams was sitting there with his Bren gun on the table, then there was the French doctor and the German naval officer whom we'd taken.

"We went down into the cellars and it was then we offered the men a choice - whether to stay behind or make a break for it, as we were now eighty metres behind the German lines, completely cut off. Williams, Crossley and three others decided they'd go and try to fight their way out. They took the German naval officer as a hostage. I fired a Verey light and the Germans thought it was their own troops and stopped shelling. I could hear Bren guns dying away in the distance.

"On the morning of June 14th we noticed a bicycle coming into the village. It was a British officer, carrying a white flag, who had been fired upon. I went out and met him. He said 'I've got a message for you. General Fortune of the Fifty-first Highland Division surrendered at St. Valery on the 12th. Your orders are to surrender. You're two days late. There's a battery of artillery, a battalion of infantry and a squadron of Stukas ready to wipe you out.' So that was it. I remember when one of the Germans saw the blackened faces of the dead in the village he said 'Have you been using Negro troops?' The German Commander said 'You're the only resistance we've met so far,' which I suppose was a bit of a compliment.

"We were put into trucks and driven east. At some point we began a great long march through Belgium and Holland with thousands of other prisoners. I had fallen off a motor-bike and got a hole in my knee and made this an excuse to get a lift now and then in a truck. You had to fiddle your way through as best you could. Finally we got to Laufen near the Austrian/German border. We went first to the Archbishop's Palace. We weren't very far from Salzburg. Some prisoners from Canada had been put in underground forts and we were going to have the same treatment meted out to us. So were were sent there too.

"In fact we were treated well. The Germans were regular Prussian Army troops. They had been given orders to give us a hard time and to force-march us, but in fact if we dropped our kits German lorries would come up behind and collect them. The guards would often connive to arrange that we could get Red Cross parcels in the normal way. They often didn't obey the tough orders they got from above. Then we had a visit from Franz Werner, the one German prisoner who escaped from Canada. He actually got us out of these underground forts to better ones at Thorns. At that time we could see all sorts of German troops moving into Russia, which was fascinating.

"We were later sent to Bibarach. Five of us tried to escape by crawling under a train but were discovered by a wheel-tapper. The Commandant had us sent off to Colditz. We shouldn't have been there at all as it was supposed to be for very hard cases, but there was actually every kind you could think of. There was Richard Grenville Herd, Dean of Peterhouse, Cambridge, imprisoned for preaching against Germans; also Yves Congar, a Dominican and eminent Roman Catholic theologian. They used to take services. There were servicemen, French, Dutch, Belgian, Polish, British; commanders from the Air Force, Army and Royal Navy; spies; high-ranking national hostages; men working out escapes; men learning each other's languages. I was in the middle of all this for four years.

"During those years my main role was drawing portraits of men in the camp, hundreds of them. I used to go to the technical college at Kendal for art, to classes paid for by K Shoes. I made portraits of prisoners and sent them home to my father, who sent them to the *Illustrated London News*. The Germans didn't mind. There was nothing controversial about them and everybody seemed happy. I got a little contribution fee from the paper and I kept the copyright which I still use.

"The Dutch had given me a handsome present of two boxes of oil paints; the thirty-six Dutchmen in camp who had been members of the Dutch Army had refused to sign a non-aggression pact with Hitler. The paints had been sent by the Red Cross. I set up my studio and was allowed extra window space. The rooms were big, maybe with fifty or sixty men in each. I got extra paints from the Germans and paint was sometimes borrowed from me.

"Now here is an interesting thing. After forty-five years the B.B.C. became interested in what had happened at Colditz. Years after the war they had heard from the Dutch that I had supplied paints which they had used for painting the faces of dummies which the Dutch had substituted for the faces of prisoners who had escaped. At the time I was unaware the Dutch were using the paints for this purpose. I didn't know about it until, as I said, years later through the Dutch telling the B.B.C.. The Germans came around and saw me painting every day - they saw how upset I pretended to be if any of my stuff was touched.

"We had in the camp the world's leading forger of postage stamps. All sorts of documents were forged in the camp and sometimes I had to match colours. We'd maybe have a pass from a German guard by giving him cigarettes. We'd put it on a table with the experts all round it and we would examine the text, the title, the quality of the paper and I would match the colours. The guard would be pacing outside the door hoping he wouldn't get caught.

"Our liberation was a great event. We noticed the Flying Fortress coming over, a wonderful sight. Then came fighter bombers, then shelling began. We heard the German tanks radioing to each other 'Attention, attention, English tanks.' Then we heard the American tank commanders talking to each other. The Germans blew up the bridge over the River Mulde and some in the camp were blown off their chairs. Douglas Bader and a few others were knocked off their legs.

"Eventually a detachment came up and began to hammer on the

outer door. We rushed down but a German officer stood with his back to the gates even though the Americans were on the other side. 'Get back from these gates' he shouted. We all stopped, some, indeed, admiring this man's bravery, doing his duty right up to the last minute. But the Americans came in. We looked awful compared with them; they were front-line troops, big, bearded chaps and we were like skeletons. We were allowed into the village. I was given a stint of duty with a whistle around my neck.

"Everything was a bit chaotic. Some did good things like helping to repair the waterworks. Others did a bit of looting, thousands of cigarettes. Some got hold of superb motor-bikes. There was no order at all. Hundreds of women queuing outside shops. One small girl came up to me and asked me if I'd buy her some coffee. She handed me the money and coupons and said 'You are the conquerors, you don't need to queue.' I suppose she gave me my first lesson in the conqueror's power. She asked me to move dead bodies from the lawn of her home.

"This was April 16th and I was flown back to England two days later. I was on the books of K Shoes but I was given a sabbatical in London and I went to the Slade School. I spent some time convalescing at Glencorse in Edinburgh. There was nothing wrong with me but the Army was making sure they didn't need to pay me a disability pension. In the end I came back to the Advertising Department at K Shoes in Kendal.

"The portraits I had done were historically, not academically interesting. My chief hobby is portrait painting and if people want them, I sell them. I take a photograph of the person, then I do a drawing. If they want an original, they can buy it. I did one of Vincent Massey, the High Commissioner for Canada, and also Elie de Rothschild. He joked about joining the ranks of the unemployed because Mitterand had confiscated his bank which was worth millions.

"My faith has meant a lot to me. I saw many dreadful sights during the war, but in war you expect them. I'm more shattered if I see someone under the wheels of a motor-car than dead bodies on the battlefield. During the war we had a padre who was a brother of Cardinal Heenan, he'd hear my confession when I was sitting on a motor-bike! I remember in Poland we were without a priest, but all of a sudden in came a German bishop who was a colonel in the Wehrmacht. He swept into where the prisoners were. He said mass. He was a real bishop who cut through the formalities and off he went.

"I've had a pleasant life living and working in Cumbria."

JOE BRADBURY

Working with Paper

"Both my wife and myself had an interesting start in life. I started off in Marylebone workhouse. I was born in 1910 and came to the South Lakeland area as a baby. After a bit I was put into the orphans home at Natland. It isn't run as an orphans home now but is for deprived children and for holidays and that sort of thing. I was there for two years, then they fostered me out again to Burneside where I am still. I lived with a Mr and Mrs Davies.

"My dear wife was in a similar position to me; she started off life in a home for girls. It's now a home for old people. She was there till she was sixteen, then she went as the under-nurse to the Cropper family. The family owned the famous paper works at Burneside. At that time when my wife was sixteen, in 1923, James Winstanley Cropper, the third generation of Cropper and Co., was head of the firm. Nora my wife helped his wife, Marjorie. They had a head nurse and she was the assistant. When the head nurse left to get married, Nora took over.

"We got married in 1935 and have celebrated our golden wedding. We've had two daughters and now have six grandchildren and five great-grandchildren. So you see we've been very fortunate in life.

"I went to school in Burneside and, when I left, my first job was in Cropper's Paper Works and I was there for fifty-one years. I started as what we called then a 'cutter boy.' A cutter would cut the reams of paper into sheets and the cutter boy would put the shavings into bags. I got 13/6d a week for that job. That was in 1924. I worked actually at Cowan Head, the mill about a mile and a half up the valley, but it's closed now and all operations are carried on at Burneside. There was another mill operating up the valley at Bowston but it's closed down too.

"After being a cutter boy I went on to work at the paper-making machine at Cowan Head. Then I came down to Burneside to work on a paper-making machine there. There were four machines at Burneside and I was on number two machine. After that I went on to work in the Salle, the finishing room where the paper is packed, and eventually I became foreman there. At that time there would be about thirty girls in the Salle. They sorted out the papers, but nowadays it's mostly done by machine.

"In 1939 I went out to France with the local Border Regiment. We were the first territorial battalion in France. We managed to get out after Dunkirk and landed home at Southampton on June 17th. Soon we were sent out to the Middle East. We went to the Western Desert, then on to Lebanon where the trouble is now. We disarmed the Vichy French in Syria when they capitulated. That would be 1942. Then we came back down to the desert and thought we were going home, but we were sent to Tobruk which was under siege at the time. At that time they were sending the Australians out because their country was threatened by Japan. We were in Tobruk until the Eighth Army came up to Tobruk to break the siege. We went out to meet them.

"I was a sergeant at the time. I was in charge of an anti-tank platoon with an officer. We followed the troops out but ran into land mines. I was on the truck when it blew up. I got a hole in the side of my head near my eye and it affected my sight for a few weeks. They sent me down to a Cairo hospital. I was very lucky because the boat I should have sailed on got sunk. I couldn't get on it because it had a full complement. Our drum major in the Border Battalion was on it and was drowned. I was in hospital when the battle of Alamein started up.

"They got us together again and sent us off to India, and we went off for jungle training for the Burma job with the Chindits. During the jungle training I became infected with phlebitis and other things, so they sent me up to the hills to do a job up there, then down to the transit camp where I was six months as a quarter-master sergeant. We came back in January 1945 and I went back to Cropper's and, after a little time, was a foreman again in the Salle. I stayed there till I retired in 1975. It's been wonderful after the start my wife and I both had.

"Paper-making is a very interesting industry. Cropper's has been on the go since 1845 when James Cropper at twenty-two years of age began the business, and it has been in the family ever since. Water is very important in paper-making because wood pulp fibres, from which paper is made, bond together in water. Cropper's got water from reservoirs in Potter Fell. Over five million gallons a day went through the paper machines at that time. Two of our four machines produced glazed paper. The paper was wound, laminated for boards, coated and embossed. Today all sorts of chemical and fibrous materials are used in paper-making.

"There are all sorts of uses for the paper made at Cropper's. There are wove and fine coloured papers. Dyestuffs are very important for this side of paper-making. There are also stationery products, printing paper and board, paper for catalogues, products for packaging, bookbinding products and papers used in different industries, absorbent paper, oil impregnated manilla, manilla for tickets and tags, hundreds of uses. What would we do without paper?

"In my day paper was made mostly from waste paper and wood pulp, now a lot of the waste cames from computer waste and buff cuttings from envelope factories. Most of the pulp came from Scandinavia, but some came from the U.S.A. and Canada and places like Spain, Portugal and Brazil. By the time I came to make paper the use of rags was finished.

"With the use of machines and new technology there are fewer people working at Cropper's now although production has increased. As I said, in my time there were actually about thirty girls and about thirty men in the finishing department, but machines now do a lot of the work. It hasn't affected the village really as much of it has come about through natural retirement.

"The Cropper family has always had a connection with Burneside. My wife of course, as their nurse, was close to them since she was sixteen. The home Nora had been in was a domestic training home and she was very lucky to go to the Croppers, for she found them a lovely family. It was her first real home. James Winstanely Cropper was head of the family then and his wife was Marjorie, she was a Bagot from Levens Hall. It was his grandfather who had started the business in 1845. They had five girls and a boy. The present chairman, James, is the grandson of the family my wife worked for. There's always been a Cropper at Burneside. Charles James Cropper, the second generation of Croppers, died soon after my wife went to work there. The family now live at Tolson Hall off the Windermere road. My wife enjoyed her work with Mrs Marjorie Cropper who was really like a mother to her. The girls came to our golden wedding; two, who really were almost my wife's babies, have died since then.

"I remember in the old days in Burneside there was what you might call a burial club. The lady who brought me up was in it. When anybody died they used to collect a shilling from all the other members and that helped to pay for the funeral. There wasn't an awful lot of money in those days. When we married I had £2.12s each week to live on. We got one of Mrs Cropper's cottages to let. We paid half-a-crown a week in rent. It was just up the fields there. There were at that time no mod cons, we had to go to a well for water and the lavatory was outside - no water flow, you had to empty your own bucket! We had six years there and then we came down into Charles Court, just opposite the school. These houses were built in memory of Charles Cropper. Where we're living now is called Churchill Court because it was completed by Cropper's just after the end of the war. Now as houses fall vacant they are sold. Latterly my wife, who is now eighty-one, used to go back and babysit for the family. They've kept in contact. The Croppers are very good to their old workers, as well as the pension of course, they give everybody £20 at Christmas.

"There have been differences from the little old village of Burneside over the years. To our age group and our way of thinking it has overgrown itself. There are now two big council estates. Before it was just Cropper's houses and the houses round the village. In my day, where the shops are now it was all green fields. We had a co-operative then and a cobbler's shop that sold sweets and newspapers. The cobbler was a 1914-1918 war veteran with just one leg. When he died his widow kept the paper side going for a bit. Now we have Spar and a baker's and of course the post office where you can also get groceries - three shops.

"I've had a busy life. I was on the Church Council and in the choir for fifty-nine years. I was on the Parish Council and also on the School Board where I was secretary and one of the managers. I sing with the Burneside Choral. I was in the K Shoes Choir in Kendal. I was also in the famous Greenside Choir, we went to the Albert Hall and won the all-Britain competition. I sing tenor. Nora has been busy too. We're both in the over sixties group. Nora has been in the Mothers' Union all her married life and the British Legion. Yes, we've had a lovely life in Burneside."

PERCY DUFF M.B.E.

Town Treasurer

"I started at sixteen in Kendal in the borough treasurer's office not as *a* junior clerk but as *the* junior clerk in 1938. It was a condition when you came into the office that you would agree to study for the accountancy exam. I had done part of that when the war came along and I was away for five years. I finished my accountancy exam when I came back. I took the rating and valuation exams. The Rating and Valuation Association exams were important for the office, in addition to being an accountant. Then I just worked up in the office till I became the chief accountant. Mr Wainwright who is famous for his books on the Lake District was my boss. I had been a trainee under him so I've known him since 1941. In fact I've known him longer than anyone in Kendal and still visit him regularly. When he retired in 1967 I became the borough treasurer.

"I stayed as the borough treasurer until after the reorganisation of local government, then the title was altered to the town treasurer. I went to be the housing accountant with the District Council. I retired officially five years ago. I still retain the ancient office of town treasurer, I have an office in the town hall and still go in some days of the week because I look after a very big voluntary housing charity. That's really why I've been given this office as I couldn't keep all the documents and cabinets at home. This is the housing charity, called the Mayor of Kendal's Charity for the Homes of the Aged and Infirm, I've just finished a quarter of a million pounds scheme of flats and bungalows. I look after things like that from here. We've thirty-nine modern properties all paid for. So that's kept me out of mischief. I don't get paid for this but I feel it's one way of giving something to the community.

"I was born and bred in Kendal. I went to St. Thomas' Primary School and then with a scholarship on to the local grammar-school which was different in those days as there were only one hundred and twenty of us there. I lived up at Kendal Green so we had the green to play on at football and cricket. There was comparatively less traffic in those days so you went on your bicycle. In fact my reward for passing the scholarship was that Father got me a bicycle, other successful pupils got bikes too. The old grammar-school is now called Kirkby Kendal School, along past Netherfield. It was founded in 1525.

"In 1938 when I started, it was just as difficult to get a job as it is now. Eleven of us came along for an interview. I was lucky to have been top of the school in maths at that time. I was always good at maths but I couldn't pass in French. Anyway, I got the job.

"I've always been interested in motor-cycling. I've served on the General Council of the Autocycle Union which is the motor-cycle branch of the R.A.C.. I used to go down to London to the R.A.C. meetings. I'm still the treasurer for the area and I'm president of the local motor club which is one of the oldest motor clubs in the country, founded in 1910. In fact I wrote its history when it was seventy-five years old.

"I've got another great interest which really springs from what my wife has done. She has published a book of photographs of old Kendal. If I quote what she says in the preface to the book it perhaps explains it better. This is what she says, "My interest in old photographs of Kendal started in 1970 when I was preparing a photographic record of the activities of the Westland Motor Club founded in 1910. In addition to giving me photographs of motor-car activities many people gave me old pictures of Kendal. When reorganisation of local government came about in 1974, there was a tendency to forget about old records. However my husband was able to ensure that the glass plate negatives of old pictures, and other photographic material recorded in the Kendal offices, were saved from destruction for the people of Kendal. Since 1974 our joint interest has become widely known, as a result many photographs have been handed to us for safe keeping. The collection has now reached considerable proportions and to enable the people of Kendal to share our good fortune we've given slide shows and exhibitions. The response of local people has been most rewarding."

"Princess Anne came to open our exhibition of photographs at the Brewery Centre in Kendal. She talked for about ten minutes with my wife who showed her round the exhibition. We had just got the new gallery at the Brewery, they thought the town should have a non-controversial exhibition to open it and they asked us if we'd put it on. The plaque says it was opened by Princess Anne.

"There is a tremendous interest in old Kendal. If I put a film show on in the town hall, it's packed. I've done a number of slide shows and there's great interest shown. This kind of interest is growing, the books that are being published on communities in days gone by prove it. There is a market for them, not an unlimited market, but an economic one.

"My wife first got the idea that, as no one else had done the history of the motor club, she would do it. So she put a letter in the local paper saying she was going to do this and photographs came in from all over, including Bulawayo. So you can see how far the local paper gets to! The history now runs to five volumes with marvellous photographs. She has actually left it in her will to go to the archives.

"Then people started giving us other photographs of old Kendal and I've got all the glass plate negatives stored here and they belong to the town. They were taken in the latter part of the last century. I've got all kinds of pictures here, old street scenes, early photographs of the police and so on.

"All this interest in old Kendal spread from the photographic side into the history side. I was particularly interested in the Council's activities and local government activities over the years. Our first charter was granted in 1189 by Richard the Lion Heart for a market on Saturdays, and we've had a market on Saturdays ever since. I'm going to try to persuade the Council to have some sort of celebration in 1989 when we'll have had a market for 800 years. Richard the Lion Heart was on his way to the crusades at the time and he was short of money - kings were always short of money. The Baron of Kendal was with him and he crossed the king's hand with silver and so Kendal got its charter. Our incorporation as a borough came along in 1575 from Queen Elizabeth I. Catherine Parr who married Henry VIII was born here in the castle.

"The life of Kendal has been bound up with its industries as well as with administration. It was founded on the woollen industry. Last century of course the leather and shoe industries developed. When the industrial revolution came about the main woollen industries moved largely to Yorkshire with the development of the big factories there, although in the nineteenth century we had several mills in Kendal. Of course when we exported our woollen goods to America tobacco came back, and tobacco was ground up to make snuff. There were three firms of snuff makers at one time. One of them had a terrific fire and it destroyed their factory. They were bought out by another firm. It was a disaster. Geoff Gawith is in the factory in Lowther Street; his father and grandfather ran it before him.

"My interest in old Kendal and its charters is of course a personal one. Miss Sheila McPherson is the official archivist for the county. Although she has an office here, she has also an office at Barrow and also at Carlisle.

"I never appreciated how important it was to preserve the old records until the reorganisation of local government came along. I had worked for the Town Council all my life, reorganisation was the end of local government as I had always known it. There was now much more central government interference and control. Politicans of all parties must accept responsibility. We have retained, in contrast to what you hear happening in some extreme councils, an air of common-sense here. Although the Town Council lost a lot of its powers when reorganisation took place, there was a special dispensation which applied to us. Boroughs of more than twenty thousand people were supposed to go out of existence. Kendal and some others, by an Act of Parliament, were allowed to continue as Town Councils, the voice of the people at grass roots level. They also administer things like allotments, lighting, bus shelters, local details right down to litter bins. In our case we retained a lot of local ceremony which I find interesting.

"We have many official visitors from overseas and the mayor entertains them in his parlour. When the mayor takes over for a year, he takes over the mayor's parlour and that's his room during the year of office. He is expected to entertain all official visitors to the town. Of course he gets an allowance which enables him to do this, a grant to cover his expenses. This lets a working man carry out the duties, which is a great thing as otherwise you'd get an ordinary working man, a good councillor, well respected in the community, but because of his financial position he couldn't take the office. Everybody should have the right to be mayor if he or she is capable of it.

"In the mayor's parlour we keep the town's treasures, e.g. the borough charter which I mentioned before and which came along in 1575. With that charter came the right to have two maces, always in front of the mayor when he went out on official business. (The two maces we have now were made in 1647. On the maces are the emblems of England, Scotland, Ireland and France, because the Queen at that time was said to claim to be Queen of France.) This charter was bought for the sum of £137-19s-5d. It was raised by door to door collection. Contributions were received from fourpence to forty shillings.

"Another treasure in the mayor's room is a seal from Queen Elizabeth I in 1576, that seal is used on all official documents although we don't use that actual original seal. I've got one here that we use for routine use.

"Now we've got a second charter here from King Charles I, and that one gave us the right to have a sword and official sword-bearer from the sovereign. He preceded the two mace bearers. Many towns have bought swords but we have the right to carry a sword because of that charter from King Charles I in 1636. Later we got another charter in 1684 from King Charles II. Kings were always short of money and this was one way of raising it, by granting a Charter of Incorporation.

"The silver maces, sword and seals are kept in a chest in the mayor's parlour. When we get official visitors they're there for them to see as well as the royal charters. And of course the townspeople can come along and see them too, as they don't belong to the mayor or anyone else, but to the town. Also in the parlour are several items of silver that have been given to the town over the years. Another item is Queen Catherine Parr's prayer-book which was purchased in 1936 for £500. How much it would be worth if the Americans got the chance to buy it I just wouldn't know!

"There had been an antiques fair in London and an antiques dealer from Kendal was down there. The dealer who was selling it could have let it go to America but he said to our dealer from Kendal 'I'll let it go for £500.' So the Kendal man rushed back here and a public appeal was launched and we bought it. It's now in a lock-fast safe built into the wall. It's not handled because it's very fragile but it's there for all to see. Many of the prayers in it were copied out by an expert when the parish church was celebrating their nine hundred years. They're now in book form which the parish church sells for £1.00 to raise funds for the church. It is beautifully illustrated.

"I feel strongly there is a place for the traditional ceremonies and symbols of the local government heritage. I deplore the disregard some extreme councils have for that honourable heritage, such as wanting to dispense with the personage of a mayor. Here the mayor is a greatly respected figure and his office is respected, his duties are numerous and occasions are enhanced by his presence. We feel Kendal was incorporated as a community through its charters and seals of incorporation and the symbols and ceremonies mean somelthing that's real in the history and spirit of the town. Maybe I'm biased but that's how I feel.

"To celebrate our centenary in 1875 we decided to purchase a chain for the mayor which was solid gold, the money was raised by public subscription. At the same time a jewel was purchased to hang round his throat for when he goes out to official dinners and such like when he can't wear the chain, he wears the jewel at his throat instead. The mayoress's chain was purchased at the time of King George VI's coronation in 1937. Now, there's no such person as a mayoress in law officially, but of course we've always had one. Because of the emancipation of women from the 1920's onwards the role of women became more and more important and she got invited out to many places on her own, as a lady in her own right, such as to Townswomen's Guilds, W.I.'s or the schools and so on. There are many organisations now who may not want the mayor but just the mayoress!

"There may be one snag here; you have a mayor who is used to public speaking as a councillor but sometimes a wife has had no experience at all in public speaking. So when someone is invited to be mayor, especially nowadays with so many public duties, he has to take into account whether his wife is happy about taking on the expected duties of the office where she has to perform on her own. Not everyone may want to. Anyway our mayoress has a lovely gold chain of her own which she wears on her many official visits.

"In my own job I became, through long experience, somewhat expert in housing matters. I felt the housing duties of the old Borough Council were most important. I was interested in providing accommodation especially for the older people. When the government was considering the right-to-buy legislation I was asked to appear before the sub-committee in the House of Commons. They wanted some advice on the sale of properties in the Lake District and National Park.

"As time went on I gradually became interested in voluntary housing, especially the Mayor of Kendal's Homes for the Aged. Voluntary housing, which is a movement throughout the country, provides houses in addition to the provision by local authorities. In 1947 when this particular Kendal charity started, the money was just raised by local people by giving their property, leaving their money or by coffee mornings and all sorts of ways like that. But the particular charity I'm responsible for now, and which is a very substantial housing charity, is adequately financed. Over the last few years the government has taken a great interest in charities which make provision for the elderly. There are now Acts of Parliament which assist housing associations and, as a registered housing association, we've had a lot of assistance.

"It is very well known in this area that in the Mayor's Charity for Homes for the Aged, very little money goes for administration. The secretary and I run the charity. I'm the treasurer and correspondent.

111

We just get our expenses such as telephone calls. I say this because I don't want people who have questions about some charities pointing a finger and saying 'You do all right out of that.' I simply feel we should do a little bit for our communities.

"In my long career in local government there have been great changes. When I came here as office boy, the old Borough Council used to do gas, electricity, water, maternity and child welfare, police, education. My own feeling is that the reorganisation in big units which took place in 1974 destroyed true local government. It took government further away from people themselves. I think in time there will be a reversal and things will come back in terms of greater involvement of people. There is, I believe, a possibility that powers like education and the police will move away from local government as it is now, but that local concerns like parks or rubbish collections or that sort of thing will stay within real local government. That of course is only my opinion.

"I'm sorry politics has crept into local government in the way it has. You get it at county and district level, even at town council level. For instance, in the discussion of small things like allotments; there is a tendency, which is quite ridiculous, for people to vote on party lines when every decision should be in the interest of Kendalians. In this tendency there is the chance of local government ultimately cutting its own throat.

"I've had a happy life in Kendal and there's nowhere I'd rather be. When, years ago, I passed my accountancy exams, Mr Wainwright said 'There's no vacancy at present for a qualified accountant. You'd better look round and see what vacancies are available elsewhere.' I had a look at the *Local Government Chronicle*, the magazine where all the adverts appeared. There was only one advert for a qualified accountant and that was in a Lancashire town and I thought 'No way am I leaving Kendal for that.' But things worked out and Kendal it was to be for the next half century."

JOE FAUGHEY

Making Biscuits in Carlisle

"I was born in Carlisle and went to St. Bees School which was practically opposite Carr's factory. Then I went to St. Patrick's Secondary School. I left at fourteen. Within two weeks I started work in Carr's biscuit factory and I worked there for fifty-one years, 1934 till 1985.

"Carr's is famous for its biscuit-making all over Britain. The man who started it was Jonathon Dodgson Carr away back in 1831. In that year he walked all the way from Kendal to Carlisle and started up a bakery in Castle Street. He built a flour mill in Church Street where the factory is today. There was a small bakery beside the mill where he made bread and cakes too. His hand-made biscuits were popular. He must have been a clever man for he designed and put into his factory the first biscuit cutting machine. That was the first of the Alphabet biscuits known to children in this country.

"When I joined they trained me to wrap biscuits. Boys and girls from school-leaving age were given this type of job - what you called a 'tupenny packet', a small packet of biscuits all hand-packed. It was in a kind of grease-proof paper with a design on it, Carr's of Carlisle and the name of the product.

"We had lots of brands then - Rich Tea, Abernethy, Marie, Cherry Walnuts, Cream Cakes, Butter Puffs, Cumberland Cracker, and so on. The processes of making them are much the same today, but they are much more automated; that's the main difference. The machines basically haven't changed in the last fifty years. Of course some areas of biscuit-making, like dough-mixing, have advanced because of technology and computers. In those days it was all sack materials that were brought in - sack flour. At that time I think most of it would come from Silloth which was then a subsidiary of Carr's but there was a breakaway, I think in the early nineteen-hundreds.

"There was a lot of manual work in those days. Carr's must have employed eighteen hundred to two thousand people, eighty per cent women, chiefly doing the packing. Now of course women can operate wrapping machines.

"At the end of my first week in 1934 I got eight shillings. Then you got yearly increments: the second year you went to 10/3d and then

113

to 12/6d and so on till you got a man's wage at the age of twenty-four. I worked for the five years then went into the Border Regiment in 1939.

"In those days there was a different department for making cakes - a cake bakehouse, but I wasn't involved in cakes in a significant way till after the war. I went through all the processes of biscuit-making. In 1936 I was given an apprenticeship as a biscuit-maker, a five year apprenticeship which meant I was starting from the ground floor and going through all the processes. Then came the war and after it I continued where I left off. I had learned all the processes of operating and all the ingredients needed to make biscuits; about the different chemicals and their uses during biscuit-making, like bicarbonate of soda, sodium and so on.

"When I became a journeyman I was given a biscuit cutting machine to operate in 1947, which was a step up the ladder. With this machine you could cut many different brands by changing the cutter. In 1948 I became an ovensman, then I got the job of night foreman. I got married in that same year, 1948. I married a local girl whose name was Carlisle and who also worked in the factory as a packer.

"By now progress was continuing in the factory in the concept of the travelling ovens. The idea was a travelling band, something similar to a conveyor, constantly going through a baking chamber. It's interesting in this respect to look at the meaning of the word 'biscuit'. It's real meaning is 'twice baked'. People might think that you bake it once, bring it back and bake it again, but this isn't the case. A biscuit is baked from the top and from the bottom, either baked by gas or electric heating. The biscuit travels in a tunnel or oven, right through.

"Another change was that biscuits were now stacked and run along the conveyors so girls could pick up a complete stack of biscuits, instead of picking biscuits up singly as they did pre-war. They could pick up a stack of biscuits and put them in wrapping machines or feed them into containers.

"Now that the war was over people were eating more biscuits. I think biscuits were popular because many families found cakes were a bit expensive. Pre-war cakes had not been so expensive, but after the war the price of cakes increased. A woman with a small family found she could get better value out of a packet of biscuits.

"In 1972 United Biscuits took over Carr's. There was expansion in the size of factory and more people were employed. United Biscuits is the biggest biscuit-making business in Europe. They have factories in Glasgow, Liverpool, Manchester, Harlesden in London, and Aberdeenshire, Ashby and, of course, here in Carlisle. Biscuit-making is big business involving many millions of pounds. There was great progess in Carr's as the years went on. In the centenary year of 1931 the trading profit was £69,000, in 1947 just after the war the trading profit was £167,000, in 1954 it was up to £479,000. Carr's, like many other biscuit-makers, was a family business. McVitie, Laing, Grant, McFarlane, Crawford, MacDonald - now they're one family, you might say.

"There are certain areas with special tastes. Scotland seems to be very sweet-toothed. Anything sweet in the way of biscuits, or chocolate, you put it up to Scotland.

"When I left school in 1934 it wasn't so easy to get a job in Carlisle. Young folk took whatever came along. I happened to be born in a house that belonged to Carr's. Usually the people that worked in the factory lived in the surrounding areas. You had to get to work and transport wasn't easy so people tended to live nearer where they worked. There wasn't so much moving long distances as you get today. Unfortunately at that time of the Depression a number of lads in the biscuit industry were being paid off at eighteen, so they were forced to join the Forces.

"The railway in Carlisle at that time didn't take on youngsters till they were sixteen, so that meant waiting two years after leaving school. After sixteen the railways were one of the biggest employers in Carlisle. Then there were the tin-makers which is now Metal Box. They made tins for Carr's biscuits. There was also Cummersdale print works and the print works which was run by the Chance family who owned this land our house is built on. The Chance's house is now a community centre. There was also Cowans and Sheldon, the crane-makers, who closed down last year. Their cranes were famous round the world.

"As a town Carlise has changed since I was a boy. It has expanded a lot since estates were built. Once, a mile from the town hall and you were into rural districts. Many of the houses that were council houses are now privately owned, like this one of mine. In this estate nearly all now are privately owned. The centre of the town with its pedestrian areas is greatly improved.

"I've got a son who is a section manager in Carr's. My wife retired eight years ago as a line supervisor in the firm. Between the three of us there are, let me see, fifty-one years for me, forty-six for my wife who had been a forewoman in the Chocolate Room, and twenty-four

115

for my son. We've clocked up quite a few years service to biscuit-making in Carlisle! Now my grandson is in it in the last month, doing packing. There has been a lot of family continuity in the food industry, in the MacIntosh's, the Cadbury's, the Rowntree's, the Carr's. They were strong in the family tradition. The firms knew the continuity was coming along and they knew the type of people they were getting.

"Pre-war the man's wage in the biscuit industry was 39/6d. In different types of operations, depending on what you were doing, you'd maybe get a shilling more. Being taken on as an apprentice didn't mean you were guaranteed a job for life. It meant you were given the opportunity of becoming a biscuit-maker, to continue as a journeyman if it was possible and if you wanted to. You could lose the job if you didn't show the potential.

"I went through the different grades and ended up as a manager - from night shift and day shift foreman to section manager responsible for about three hundred workers. It meant you now knew all the processes of biscuit-making from the raw materials right through to the end.

"In 1973 I was seconded to the United Biscuits factory in Jamaica. They were prepared to let our people sell their biscuits in the islands provided their own people were given the chance to make those biscuits. I went out to train them. We didn't train them in up-to-date methods, which would have been unrealistic in their situation, we trained them in basic methods which we used here twenty years before. It was like training them in the training I had had then. To train a man in how to control and develop them - for me it was a great experience.

"So there you are, the Faughey family are part of Carlisle and its biscuit-making tradition. Myself, my wife, her sister and brothers, my son and grandson - that says a lot for Carr's of Carlisle."

GEOFF GAWITH

Snuff and Tobacco Manufacturer

"I have been in the tobacco industry and in the manufacture of snuff all my working life in Cumbria. I was born in 1922 and entered the business when I was fifteen. My father had been managing director of the firm here in Kendal with the family name of Gawith. I came straight from leaving school. I learned all the various processes connected with tobacco, beginning with the manufacturing processes in our works in Lowther Street and also down at our snuff mill at Helsington Lathes.

"I have my own theory why the snuff industry started up here in Cumbria. Kendal was one of the woollen towns. Kendal cloth was wool-packed over the Lake District fells to the west Cumbrian ports and much of it was sent out to the West Indies. Tobacco was transported back to Kendal, so Kendal became a barter area. We had the tobacco here and we had the right climate, moist with a lot of rain and also a fast flowing river for power, the River Kent. At one time there were forty mills on the Kent, mills with water-power producing different things, meal, cloth and so on. We still have our water-wheel down at Helsington Lathes.

"We get our tobacco leaf from India, Canada, Malawi, Zimbabwe, Cyprus and South Africa. On the snuff side we now tend to buy scrap for, after all, we're going to grind it up. You get the scrap a lot cheaper than the leaf, and these are Burley types and air-cured types. The dark types are used for tobaccos and twists. Air-cured leaves are those dried out in the sun in the country where they are grown. Burley is a different kind of tobacco seed.

"The snuff industry in Cumbria goes back to about 1750, probably a few years earlier, but we have no records as to who was milling at that time. Then in 1792 Samuel Gawith started up and we, Gawith Hoggarth & Co. Ltd., started up in 1857. You have now the two snuff firms in Kendal, Samuel Gawith and ourselves, Gawith Hoggarth. There was some family connection of brothers who split up. In England there are only two snuff manufacturers in Sheffield and two in Kendal. It used to be manufactured in Scotland but not now. All the old machinery here came from Scotland.

"My father took over in 1914 and there have been developments

117

since then. When we started manufacturing snuff all the snuffs were the damp, coarse ground type, over fifty per cent water-logged, all cheap and nasty I'd say. These have been replaced by the finer ground snuffs which really originated in Sheffield, and we followed suit. Now our snuffs are the finer ground, dry snuffs. On the tobacco side most of the sales were twists and shags, but the shag trade dropped considerably. That was because when the railways opened up in the north, the manufacturers in the south penetrated here with their greater selling potential and that caused decrease in our sales at that time. But as time went on twist sales increased and shag sales too became considerably higher. Shag is really fine cut tobacco that's used in pipes and cigarettes.

"The start of the story is when the leaf is grown and cured in the tobacco-producing countries. It then goes on to the auction floors and we have companies out there buying for us from the auction floors. It's then shipped to this country. There's nine per cent moisture in the case of the snuff leaf - we don't mind how much that's broken as it's to be ground - and fourteen per cent in the better leaves we are going to use for tobacco. When it arrives in Britain it goes into bond in a warehouse in Manchester. We have a warehouse here in Kendal but we don't hold it all, so we draw from a warehouse in Manchester.

"When the leaves come in here they're blended. The blenders don't serve an actual apprencticeship. They learn from their own experience and from others. Altogether we employ about forty men and women, here and down at the mill.

"After this, moisture is added to the blend, we moisten it with water in bunkers and with experience our staff can tell the percentage of moisture in it. Then we add some mild preservatives to increase its shelf life. For twist it goes to the Spinning Room where it's spun in the shape of long ropes. For cut tobacco it goes through a cutting machine. When it's cut it's under pressure, so it's put into a heated drum which loosens it and it's spread out on trays to cool. We sell the great majority of tobacco in this country and export less than five per cent.

"On the snuff side we draw the leaf from our warehouse in Kendal and it's blended. It's ground with pestels and mortars. The manufactured design of the snuff pestles and mortars, a bank of four, is identical and they are all run off a cental column. After grinding to a certain point, which the operators can tell from the sound of the mill, the leafy parts are ground beautifully but the stem doesn't grind quite as fine, so the mixture is sieved to take the stem out. The stem is then put into another pestle, a metal one, which can grind the stem up fine. then the two are blended together again. That method is for the coarser snuffs.

"For the finer snuffs there are other types of mills, such as ball mills which are metal drums with soft steel balls inside and which keep pounding away - the kind that are used in the stone-grinding industry. The output of these was not sufficient so we installed the hammer mill, which really pulverises rather than grinds the stem. It pulverises it fine, but has a different finish to it because it is pulverising rather than grinding. We use both kinds of mills.

"Basically the snuff is ground tobacco and salts, which are added at the finishing part of the grinding. The salts in the main are common salt, sodium carbonate, sodium bicarbonate, potassium carbonate. Snuff without salt is like potato without salt. All this is done at the mill, then it's shipped up to the works for a final blending.

"We produce nine distinct varieties of snuff here which are different in colour, texture or moisture. We blend again from those nine basic varieties and add different perfumes so the permutations are endless. In fact we do about sixty snuffs with different flavours and different price tags - such as Wallflower, Raspberry, Aniseed, Coffee, etcetera.

"What about the people who take snuff? Miners were always the biggest single section of people taking snuff. Not just coal-mining, but any mining where there is dust. They are not allowed to smoke for danger of explosion so they take snuff or chew twist or chewing gum. Snuff-taking was common in all industries where there was dust, for instance in the old jute factories. Of course modern air conditioning and dust extractors are now used in many of the older industries. Three years ago the miners' strike resulted in closures of many mines. Since the miners strike snuff sales have dropped alarmingly.

"There used to be an awful lot of women took snuff, particularly old women. That has tended to drop. When I used to go round the shops for orders, very often there would be some old lady sitting there quietly, not saying what she wanted. The man behind the counter would tell me afterwards that she had come in for snuff, but old ladies like her wouldn't ask for it if there was someone else in the shop.

"Quite a number in the farming industry took snuff. The Army was also a traditional place for snuff and still is to some extent, especially the officer class. Also people in the Law Courts took it. You don't see it so much taking place now. I know, personally, friends and aquaintances who take it but you never see them doing so - except maybe at an occasional party. But as far as snuff-taking was concerned, naturally it tended to be in heavy industries and it was probably evenly distributed throughout the country. Today you don't see many people openly taking snuff in the way you did in earlier centuries, but there is still a good market for it. For me it has been a specialised but interesting industry and I've enjoyed my time in it."

JAMES BLANEY

Coal Miner

"I was born in Whitehaven in 1922. The colliery where I worked was beside the sea up in the Kells area. The workings were underneath the sea. It was a big colliery in those days with a few hundred men working in it, in shifts of course. It was the Haig colliery started in 1914, called after Earl Haig. From up on the pit top where they used to take tubs you could see right up to Scotland. If you were walking down the slope and slipped, you would fall right onto the beach.

"I had four sisters and one brother who was the youngest gaffer to take over all the boys and lassies who worked on the surface. He was called up during the war and was in Rangoon and Burma. So many men who worked underground were being called up that the situation got serious. They were finding difficulty in replacing these men so we got a lot of conscientious objectors who refused to go into the Services and many of them went down the pits. They didn't like the work, but to us it was our living.

"My grandfather, my father, his brother, myself and my son were miners born and bred. You see all round this area of Whitehaven there was very little else for lads leaving school. Life was hard for the miners. People nowadays don't realise there were soup kitchens. In schools too, of course, there were no such things as canteens. At school we got half an hour to go home for food and get back again.

"I went to Coach Road School, our local Catholic school. There was strict separation of girls and boys, they never sat together. If you were caught talking to a girl you got caned. The lassies stayed in their bit and the lads in theirs.

"I left school at fourteen and got a job as an errand boy in an ironmonger's shop dealing with parcels. But I was only there six months. At that time, for unemployed lads they used to have a big place down town where you went, say, at ten o'clock till the afternoon. There was a schoolmaster in charge. The idea was to keep lads off the street. There were things to do like joiner work and P.T. and you got a free bottle of milk. Some of the boys when one o'clock came would go home, but they never said anything to you.

"At sixteen my brother got me a job at the pit. As I said, he was

121

gaffer up top. I had to shove tubs and do odd jobs. Then after a spell on top I got the chance to go underground. I really went underground for more money, to give support to my father and mother. Up top I got 5/11d a week in a little brown bag. When I went underground I got 18/4d a day. I became then more or less the main support of the house as my father had to retire and my sisters got married. I handed over any earnings to my mother. I say when you lose a mother, you lose the best friend in the world.

"You got 18/4d a day for one of the hardest jobs. You had to drive main roads through stone and metal. Once you got to an end the men used to follow that way, then cut off right and left to the various places they went to work. We'd bore holes in the rock and fire it with gunpowder. It was hot work and all we had on was a pair of shorts and a vest. The back of your hands and knees were red, shovelling the stuff into tubs - real bloody hard work for 18/4d a day. Six years I was on nightshift constant and still supporting my father and mother.

"You went down to the pit bottom in the cage. There were twenty-two in it and they went down two hundred fathoms for the workings were under the sea. Once we got out of the cage we walked about fifty yards. Then there was a ride with four coaches which took you four miles. It was pulled by an electric engine. When you got out there was a deputy waiting. He tested your lamp before you went to the workings. It was so steep to get up you couldn't walk up it, so they put a man-riding belt in. You got on at the bottom and lay on it on your belly and you went up about five hundred yards to the top. It didn't go fast. Then when you got off you had an hour's walk to the place you were working at. While you were walking, it wasn't natural air, it was compressed air worked with big fans, yet it was very very warm.

"I had a bottle of water and two rounds of bread. Some put jam on, I always took cheese. Once you took your clothes off the mice used to go through your shirt. When you went for a drink of water or maybe fancied a tit-bit, you'd find the mice had got at the bread and there were holes in your clothes. The mice would run round you when you were working. By this time when I was working at the face, I had done about twenty-five years making roads.

"You got an extra 5/- working at the face. You would take a length of sixteen feet, what they called a stint. The bulk man with tape and chalk measured sixteen feet and marked it. You had to take that sixteen feet off at £2-10s-0d a shift, then you'd move into another stint. We had four or five little cutting machines between ten men -

like a machine with a pick in it. You had to wait for each man to load a lot of his coal down. While he was clearing that up and getting it onto the belt you had the use of the machine, which loosened the coal and you got it on the moving belt and it went out-by. It was hard work, those days before the big coal-cutting machine came in.

"We sucked tobacco, so much water came out of the body with the work and heat. It was very very stewy. No electrics were allowed up to, I think, the last seven years I worked down the pit, as there was so much gas. At the William colliery there had been a number of terrible explosions. There are still thirteen bodies somewhere down the pit I worked in over a period of years. They were never recovered. If there was a lot of gas and an explosion they rushed a concrete mixer down the pit with sand, cement and bags. They used to work the clock round, the men never stopping work, mixing the concrete, putting it in small bags that you carried on your shoulder and you'd maybe go in thirty yards where it was red hot. The bags were piled one on top of the other, right across until the entrance was blocked up. The dead bodies were behind that. They worked the clock round and as you went in with the bags the sweat was running down. There was no hope for the lads blasted in the explosion.

"Conditions improved when they brought in pit-head baths about 1940. My father always bathed at home in one of those tin baths. On the early shift we'd get out of bed at quarter past four. Mothers had a hard time. No bathrooms in many houses and no washing machines. Mothers scrubbed floors with a scrubbing brush. The pit-head baths were the best thing that ever happened.

"There are no working collieries left in the area but in those days there were several. There was one called Wellington and another, Ladysmith, which was flooded with water and William which was bricked-in with rubbish where they had a lot of explosions. Ladysmith and Wellington had been built up before my time. Coal-mining in those days provided more jobs than any other industry in this area.

"After nationalisation all our pits came under the Lancashire area. We got the big electric coal cutters and electric boring machines about 1970. Before it had been all compressed air. The difference was fantastic. The work was easier but we got less money. There was more tonnage with the new machinery. But you still had to work hard. The face was two hundred and fifty yards. The big machine would travel cutting as it went right up to the face, which was only two feet six inches high and you were on your knees all the time. They introduced knee-pads to protect your knees for you were going along there six times in a shift. You were crawling three times up and three time back. The coal went on to the shunt, then down to the moving belt. I had to make sure the conveyor belt was straight where the coal came down. I had to control the overhead chocks that supported the roof, let them drop not more than six inches. When stones came down you thought the world was coming to an end.

"When the coal came down the face it dropped onto the belt which would take it to the belt on the main road. This was a special belt, forty-two inches broad, that would take the coal the four miles you had come in on the riding. From the pit bottom the coal went up a chute and on the surface it was put into tubs. They went up what they called a creeper to the pit tops. A tumbler turned them round and the coal went into the wagons.

"When I finished in 1971 I was a chargehand, in charge of more or less twenty men, a gaffer at the face. The manager paid you £5 a week extra, but for that you got a lot of impudence. Some of the lads didn't like being told what to do and could be very impudent, but mostly they were good lads. If you hadn't been on a bonus you would have been coming home with about £50 a week. That was 1971. With the bonus I could take home about £65 clear and I had started at 5/11d.

"My great hobby is pigeons. You find many miners go in for this. Again it's a hobby that comes down the generations. My grandfather and father went into this. When you've worked all your life, hard work, when you retire you've got to do something to pass the time. Another thing is my dog. I think a dog is a great thing, not only for people like me but for many who live alone. They can be a companion and go with you on your walks.

"I breed pigeons and I race them. You put your birds in a basket which goes to the west Cumbria headquarter, St. Benedict's Church which you can see from here. They are sent over to France by ferry. You come into contact with people from here down to Millom. The Barrow area has its own competitions. Our area is Carlisle to Millom and you're competing with a terrible lot of birds. I think in racing, hens are generally recognised as the best, although a fortnight ago my Auld Lad won.

"The pits as I said are now closed, but they're going ahead with opencast mining of coal. Things are uncertain but they're making preparations for it. When it gets going they'll want men with some experience of the mines, but it won't employ nearly as many men as in the old days. In Cumbria the mining of coal in pits as we knew it is dead."

JIM NOBLE M.B.E.

Journalist

"I am Jim Noble and a Kendalian. I belong to a family that was largely engaged in the shoe trade working for the Somervell brothers, manufacturers of K Shoes. I was the only member of the family who didn't follow that line.

"I went to two Church of England schools, Kirkland School in the southern part of the town and then the Central School, where at the age of twelve I won a scholarship, one of two offered to the County of Westmorland for entry to the Quaker School in Kendal, a boarding school with more than five hundred pupils. Two Kendal boys both, strange to say, with the same initials, John Nelson and Jim Noble, were the successful ones out of thirty-five who sat the examinations from schools all over the county. I think it was from there that something of my future career was worked out. I was fortunate to obtain the Classics prize, taking Latin, French and English before I left. That enabled me to get a job as a journalist on the Westmorland Gazette.

"I was nineteen when I started, in the late 1920's. There was no training scheme for journalists then, but by ensuring private tuition over six months, paid for by the authority, I became efficient in shorthand writing and typing. Kendal in those days depended upon two sources for tuition: one was a lady called Miss Cunningham who taught a tremendous number of people shorthand and typing, the other was the Allan Technical School in Kendal, now used for Further Education.

"In the office I started off reporting weddings, people's deaths or accidents. Sometimes I was sent with a senior reporter to the courts to report the court cases there. The offences generally were nothing of the magnitude in common practice today.

"Going on different reporting jobs we sometimes had a photographer with us. The photographer had to decide, if he were shown a photograph, whether it was one by the old method that could reproduce. The photograph had to be sent away and etched out onto metal. This process was carried out at Barrow-in-Furness or in Bradford. From there the picture came back as a solid piece of metal. That was the old method called flat bed printing.

"To start with I did simple jobs. I had to record out of the newspaper each week; I counted the lines for each story and recorded those in a book. The correspondent sent in his private account at the end of the month for how much he provided for the newspaper and you compared that, for accounts purposes, with the record you made week by week. You had to contribute to the dead box, that was anything about people, it went into the record and was recorded in a book. Extracts were cut out of newspapers and placed under people's headings so that when anybody died you had ready records of all they had done. The book would record the day, month and year; then the page and column so you could find the appropriate information. It was a perfect filing system, quite simple, which is just what they do today with computers. The advantage was for a young person you had to read these things, and that was part of the process of learning. I enjoyed all the work which for me was to last forty-eight years.

"But in the early thirties there was another thing on your mind. You never knew from day to day, or from pay packet to pay packet, that there wouldn't be a little note to say that, because of difficult conditions or something, your employment would terminate next Friday. That was the threat that hung over everybody. There was none of the job protection that people have today. They just took you on for a job and you were glad to have it, for there was great unemployment in the thirties.

"That led me down the path to think what I might do if the job had to cease through circumstances outside my control. From the age of seven I had shown some ability in music and had joined the parish church choir where we had three rehearsals every week and two on a Sunday. We were under great discipline and by the time I was nine I was apparently showing something more than average ability. I was taken under the wing of the organist of the parish church for piano lessons and by the time I was fourteen I was acting as assistant organist for Kendal Parish Church.

"When I was nineteen I was invited by one of the villages to assume the conductorship of a new choir for the Mary Wakefield Festival. The condition I laid down was that they had to find the members. In about eight weeks they had thirty-five members where they hadn't a choir before. This was called the Levens Choir, the village choir. So that was my introduction to the Mary Wakefield Festival, and here I am at seventy-six still conducting choirs for the festival. In the years between I've been chorus master and the

126

chairman of the festival for fourteen years. I resigned only after the centenary which was four years ago. Over the years I've been organist and director of music at Kendal Parish Church, a post I had to give up in time due to other pressures of newspaper life, having been reporter, chief reporter, then assistant editor. The responsibilities grew with the development of newspapers.

"We used to have advertisements on the front page, then we changed over to front page news: the broadsheet form rather than the modern small paper which is easily put in the pocket or carried about. It is interesting to have seen the Westmorland Gazette grow from a sixteen to eighteen pages to sometimes seventy pages. I've seen it all grow in the last fifty-five years. But all this time, as I said, my music interest had developed because one didn't know what the future would be for one's job. That's really why I studied music very deeply and earned a diploma as a teacher, then as an accompanist which is perhaps a rather rarer accomplishment. In fact I conducted different choirs, including the British Legion Choir. I had been in the Forces for six years and came back with the rank of squadron leader, so I had an interest in the British Legion.

"Due to my newspaper work I was in close contact with local government. I was persuaded to stand as a member of South Lakeland and District Council. Normally newspaper men do not get involved in this way. After seven years I became its vice-chairman, and finished in May 1987 after two years as chairman.

"I was one of the promoters of the idea that a concert hall should be provided for Kendal. The South Lakeland District Council decided to build a leisure centre in Kendal. I was asked how big the hall should be and I said it should have a seating capacity for at least eight hundred. It was decided six hundred and twenty should be the figure, but now after five years everybody knows eight hundred is the figure that is required. The reason is, that from the point of view of professional artists and how much they cost, unless you get the number of people there it's impossible to bring artists to an area where the total seating capacity cannot meet the cost. I've been the chairman of the leisure centre, which includes the concert hall, since it was opened.

"Looking back on my years in journalism, certain impressions stick in my mind. As one who did a lot of court work, there were many events that made a deep impression. One was going to Assize Courts where there were murder trials. In those days the judge put on the black cap in prounouncing sentence. I sometimes wonder whether if the present trend of violence continues we may not, at some stage in the future, be sadly forced to reinstitute some form of the ultimate punishment for certain crimes. It is a difficult problem because we're living in a different age now. Rapid speed with cars allows wrong-doers to get out of an area. People's views change as well. I'm not expressing a point of view, but I've seen both sides of the problem of crime.

"Time and again I've been in close proximity to members of the royal family. I've also met many personalities who have come here from the days of the famous Lord Lonsdale at Grasmere Sports with his canary-coloured vehicles. He was a great figure. Grasmere brought me into touch with other well-known men. For some years after the war I was organist at Grasmere Church; there I met Archbishop Temple who used to come to Grasmere every September. He liked to sit in the congregation and listen without taking part. Very often on a Sunday morning at Grasmere you'd have four bishops of the Church of England, plus the archbishop.

"You see, these men came to Grasmere when most of the tourists had gone and the schools had resumed. The countryside was lovely in early autumn. The whole pattern in the Lake District changes with the seasons. Those who preferred to have the silence and peace of this region, and the quiet to walk around, used to come when a person like the archbishop came. Now the pattern changes again with the half-term school holidays when the children are there. Then we are into still another pattern with Christmas. This has been brought about by rapid transport, everybody having a car, and hotels being more available to people all year.

"Rector Tait of Grasmere was a marvellous man. He was a great preacher and scholar. He went to America on the occasion of the Wordsworth centenary and preached in St. John's Cathedral of New York.

"Another personality was Lord Birkett who fought the battle for Ullswater against Manchester which was trying to get as many lakes as possible under its control for water purposes. I've been friendly, almost since schooldays, with Judge Temple. He was at Kendal Grammar-school as it was then. He is a Crown Court judge sitting at Liverpool. He belongs to Kendal, just up the road at Oxenholme. He lives now near Carnforth and comes back quite a lot.

"I've been friendly with many of the leading conductors, Sir Charles Groves has been a personal friend for forty years. Also Sir Thomas Armstrong, the composer, and Cecil Armstrong Gibbs who spent the war years at Windermere and did a lot of composing. I've got some of his music here that has not been published. I've had many friends among composers, adjudicators and conductors.

"Once upon a time the duty of a newspaper was to inform people in various areas where communications were poor of events involving their own relatives and friends. An area like this is largely agricultural and the local paper had a political leaning, conservative-wise. Then newspapers had to change with the changes in people's outlook. We had what I'd call more independent stand at elections, a more even course.

"The newspaper's job has changed tremendously and the influence has been television and the radio. They brought a completely new dimension into the media world. Once upon a time the daily newspapers provided information on events far away. The local newspaper was the only way of providing local information in a limited area. People forget it wasn't until, what, 1924 that we had radio in this country, and that's not very long ago in terms of communication. So the newspaper has had to change into a much more personal role, investigating. With the changing pattern of news, so far as a local authority is concerned, people are more conscious today of how their money is spent, how their rates are spent. The concentration now is much more on what local authorities are doing and what central government is doing.

"The newspapers have had to bring themselves into the local scene because people can see the national and international scene any number of times per day on the box in the corner, or hear it on the radio. And since local radio has come into being and throwaway papers, free papers, are distributed, those are factors which have greatly affected weekly newspapers. In this area we have B.B.C. Radio Cumbria which is on twenty-four hours a day, giving its news bulletins. So the newspapers have had to gear themselves almost to a different world.

"The change has been difficult but I'm glad to say those in our part of the world who made it were level headed and not too trendy. Locally they kept their head and were respected by people. In the tabloids you got an emphasis on horror and sensationalism; you got interference into people's private affairs and over-emphasis on sex. In my view this has led to a loss of standards. When you read some of the stories in certain tabloids today, you ask yourself, how much can you really believe?

"There was a maxim by those promoting a certain daily newspaper that at one time achieved a circulation of close on five million which was: 'It doesn't matter about the news, provided you serve up the story in a different way and with a different complexion from that of three weeks ago, because the public memory is so short. So give them little stories and they'll probably have forgotten they've been published before.' So we have the daily newspapers going for very short reports - not the Times or Telegraph - and as they go for snippets, so the newspapers go for massive headlines and little stuff below. People are attracted by what they see. The first thing people see when they turn over the front page is what is on page three.

"The respect for the local press is based on the fact that it has to rely on local people. The local paper is a paper of the people, for the people and by the people; if it diverts in a trendy way it will lose its character and its reason for being in existence. When you divorce your paper from you, you lose your readership and advertising and you close up. That is why the Westmorland Gazette is a highly succesful local paper, it has kept its character in the face of all the pressures.

"I was awarded the M.B.E. seven years ago for my services to music in Cumbria. I'm still very much, in my retirement, involved in journalism and writing. I do a music critic column practically every week and voluntarily edit a little magazine. I'm vice-chairman of the Parochial Church Council of Kendal Parish Church - among the largest parish churches in Great Britain - and secretary of the Trustees of Kirkland Hall and Nether Hall, formed near the church as community centres. So you see I've had a very full and interesting life.

"My wife and I have had two sons and a daughter. My wife plays the piano and sings. My daughter plays the piano, the oboe and flute. My elder son also plays the piano. So the family has this common interest in music. Music and journalism have been inseparable and my life has been a happy one."

EDWARD McINTYRE

Shipbuilding at Barrow-in-Furness

"I was born in Dalton about five miles up the road from Barrow-in-Furness. That was in 1914, the year the First World War began. I had two brothers and two sisters. I was the youngest and the apple of my father's eye. My mother had died in the influenza epidemic of 1917. My father who had been a plater in the shipyard was ill for some time. He got very ill and was sent to the infirmary in Ulverston and at that point they sent the guardians in.

"That day, remember I was eleven, I came back from school to find the guardians had locked up the house. I was at Green School at the time the guardians had locked the door; they had made an inventory of everything that was in the house and, without informing any of my family, sold off the contents including my scout gear. (My scout gear had been purchased from donations from the big houses to the church choir for singing at Christmas.) They also sold a watch which my brother had sent me from Malta. He was in the Border Regiment. He had won it in a shoot as a marksman, it was engraved "To Joe McIntyre". Canon Possilthwaite from the local church had realised the old man was ill and had sent in the guardians. I sang as second choir boy in Canon Possilthwaite's church choir in Dalton under a marvellous singing teacher, a Mr Harry whose son was first choir boy.

"In these days the town appointed guardians, some of them were business men; they sent me to the workhouse because my sister couldn't afford to take me in to live with her. To me it was pretty awful for a kid of eleven to be locked out of his own house and put in the workhouse. That day a neighbour gave me a bit of lunch and I took the cat up to my sister's at Barrow Island. The guardians - what a misnomer that was!

"After I had been two years in the workhouse the boilermakers at Vicker's shipyard gave my sister my father's superannuation which amounted to 7/6d a week in welfare. With this extra money she was able to take me in and I left the workhouse when I was thirteen. At this time she had two children of her own.

"I remember an incident when I had just come out of the work-

131

house and gone to live with my sister who was a singer and pianist. She was in St. John's Church and also in a mission they had in Stanley Road. They were rehearsing the Messiah. A local lady who was a soprano member of the choir got tonsilitis just a week before the performance. My sister said 'You can sing this,' so I sang soprano in the Messiah. It's funny how little incidents come back to mind, for by that time I was fourteen. I lived with my sister till I was twenty-two, then went into digs in Barrow.

"My brother-in-law who was a riveter got me into the riveting department at Vicker's as a catch lad at 7/21/2d to 24/- a week. By seventeen I was on 36/- a week. Before I was twenty-one I was on £2-5s-0d a week. The full tradesman's wage was £2-19s-0d a week. As soon as I was twenty-one I could join the Boilermakers' Society as a third class member holder-on. It was very hard work and it happened to be at a time when riveting of steel plates for ships was being phased out and welding of steel was coming in. I had seen what was happening. Being now a member of the Boilermakers' Society was a good thing, for when I went to see the foreman who was in charge of the welders at that time I was already in the Boilermakers' Society. So I graduated from third class to first class and became a top-grade welder. It didn't take very long for I discovered I had a natural aptitude for welding. In riveting the steel plates of a ship we worked in squads. At first I had only worked with a hand squad on the fire. With a machine squad there were three men and when one man of those three took a day off they used to go to the market to get a third man. If you didn't get a man the other two had to go home for the day. Now, instead of using rivets to join the steel sections of a ship, you held a welding rod in your hand which softened the metal with its intense heat until the separate steel plates joined or merged together in a perfect join.

"Changes were coming into the shipbuilding industry when I was starting welding. About 1936 our chief manager was Sir Leonard Redshaw, he went to Germany for some months to study the real know-how of welding. The Germans were real experts in welding by this time, they were definitely ahead of us then. It was the right time for me, for that's when they started prefabrication, welding whole sections of a ship at a time. As time went on they spent two hundred million pounds on a vast assembly hall for prefabrication. That was after I retired.

"I have been asked if welding with all the sparks flying around is dangerous. In fact it can be more dangerous for people standing around than for a skilled welder. The arc or flash is the thing that's dangerous. The welder himself has the glass shield to protect his eyes, a special glass that filters out the ultra-violet rays. A person not protected who is standing near can get a second's flash and it has a shocking effect on the eyes. A flash which affects both eyes is very painful. In my time I've had one or two myself. It's a flash, the rays from the welding arc, not an actual spark. I had hours of agony. Initially you'd go to the gatehouse where they'd give you drops in your eyes as an antidote. If you had an extra bad flash you'd go to hospital. In four or five hours after you get the drops, your eyes get better. The flash or rays actually burn the surface of your eye. You can see all right, but it's most painful.

"When you're welding or joining two plates together in a downward direction, facing downwards, the job's easy enough, but when you're welding facing upward it gets more difficult. The inside of a submarine is a curving, circular shape. Welding up that curve, climbing the hill so to speak, is difficult.

"Vickers demand one hundred per cent welding when tested. Subs that came from America had a perfection quality of nine-nine and a half per cent in the weld. Our standard was higher. If on testing you didn't get one hundred per cent, it was taken out and re-welded. The 'X-ray men', as we called them, were experts in testing, they had 'the bomb' for testing, a small unit just shaped like a circular bomb. This itself was dangerous. The rays from the bomb directed to the weld were just as dangerous as the welder's flash. The X-ray men would set the bomb in action and walk away and leave it. They usually tested at nights or at weekends when nobody else was there. The bomb was fairly close to the weld. The X-rays from the bomb would photograph any defects in the weld. There was practically no difference in welding and in examination from the day I started till I retired.

"As I said, I was born in Dalton not far from Barrow-in-Furness, but what about the town and the shipyard where I was to work for many years? Barrow used to be a Lancashire town until the early seventies but it became part of Cumbria, so Vicker's is a Cumbrian yard. When the Furness Railway was based in Barrow and iron works were set up, the population shot up. By 1866 there were about sixteen thousand people. It was in 1870 that Barrow Shipbuilding Company was also set up. In 1896 Vickers and Sons took over the shipyard. It's said they bought it for just under half a million pounds. There has been a close connection between the shipyard and the town and some streets were called after the names of ships that Vicker's have built in the past.

"A hundred years ago men came from Scotland, the north-east of England and even from Cornwall to work in Vicker's as boilermakers, shipwrights, blacksmiths and so on. It was difficult to get the men in these different unions to become one union. I suppose the work done by different workers, like the platers and shipwrights, was in some ways similar, so it seemed sensible that they should join in one union. But men were jealous of their particular skills and that brought up problems of demarcation. The platers, like my father had been, were the men who joined the steel together and formed the shape of the ship in the workshop. The shipwrights built the berth from wood and laid down the keel from a row of thick steel plate. The shipwrights joined up the sections on the slipway. Unfortunately in the history of shipbuilding there was some suspicion among members of the different crafts. But now there is the General Municipal and Boilermakers' Union, the G.M.B., to represent shipyard workers which include platers, helpers and crane drivers. However, Vicker's workers can be proud of the fine ships and warships and submarines they have built in the past.

"Vicker's is vital for the town of Barrow. I think eighty percent of the people employed in Barrow are in Vicker's. The town more or less depends on Vicker's. Smaller firms in the area also do work for Vicker's, welding and machining and so on. You might say the Ministry of Defence groomed Vicker's, for over the years it has put many warships and submarines in its way. A lot of the workers have now got shares in the firm.

"I became good friends with a girl before the war and just after the war started we got engaged. That was 1940. Then in 1941 a terrible thing happened. The Germans had been on a big bombing raid of Belfast and I suppose on the way back they ditched a landmine which killed my fiancée and all her family. That was a great shock and I think was behind me going off to find work as a welder elsewhere. I went later as a fitter to the Manchester dry dock on ship repairs. My skills were recognised there and I was put on a mobile welding unit mounted on a barge. They towed it to the Salford docks and the barge was tied up alongside the ship to be repaired. My first job was to see the chief officer and he'd tell me what needed to be repaired. Another job was working on the Guinness boats - there were about four of them which brought barrels and casks of Guinness from Dublin. We got two free pints of Guinness at lunch time. As my mate was teetotal

I got four!

"I married my present wife on December 17th 1949. I joined the Air Force for a few years before coming back to Vicker's in Barrow. There was a humorous incident happened when I was posted to Hong Kong while in the R.A.F.. My nephew Colin and his wife worked in the bank but later started a market garden business. Now in those days when you didn't get a widespread use of toilet rolls, sometimes newspaper was substituted. One day in Hong Kong I went to the toilet picked up a newspaper and guess what, it was the Barrow News, and there before me was an account of my nephew Colin being fined 5/- for going through the lights! It's a small world.

"I returned to Vicker's as a welder, often on submarine work welding stainless steel cladding onto three per cent nickel. I remember an interesting incident. You remember H.M.S. Sheffield destroyed in the war with the Argentines? When we were building the Sheffield in sections in the assembly shop we were also building two similar ships for the Argentines. There was an explosion and a fire on the bow end of one of the Argentine ships. We took the bow section of the Sheffield and transferred it to the Argentine ship where the explosion had taken place. We made a new bow for the Sheffield.

"I have many memories of famous ships built at Vicker's. I worked on the first one thousand ton tanker built in this country. Pre-war I had worked on the Illustrious and the Indomitable and the liner City of Bermuda. I was there when Dreadnought, the first nuclear submarine, was launched. You take a pride in the names of great ships you've worked on.

"When I retired from Vicker's I became a member of the Furness Retired Boilermakers' Pensioners' Association. Mr McWhinnie who had been a branch secretary of the Boilermakers' organised it about eight years ago. The membership was about two hundred and forty, all member of the Boilermakers' Society, shipwrights, boilermakers, platers and welders. In Barrow there are five branches of the Boilermakers' Society, then there's a staff branch at Vicker's and a super-staff branch, seven branches in all.

"When a man becomes sixty-five he can join our Pensioners' Association. We meet in the Labour Club where there's a concert hall. We get various speakers to come along to speak on matters of general interest, somebody

like Mr Smith the librarian. We had slide shows and Mr Smith has told us about the history and development of Barrow, with information from old records. The director of parks has also given a talk.

"When I was seventy years of age, Mr Crossfield the parks director had a little job available. Three mornings a week, Friday, Saturday and Sunday, nine gates around Burgh Park had to be opened before eight o'clock, which meant leaving home at half-past seven. I'm now seventy-three and I hope I'll go on doing this wee job till I'm eighty. I keep my eyes open for any bit of rubbish that can be picked up. Four hours each morning, eight till twelve.

"The thirteen week strike had a big effect on the town. It put a big burden on the finances of the trades unions too. We in the Pensioners' Association are supported by the Boilermakers' in Vicker's and are in the happy position of being in the black with our funds; we donated £1,000 to those deprived through the strike. Each worker used to donate 5d from his wages to the Pensioners' Association. After a shop stewards' meeting this was raised to 10p a week and a cheque goes every month to the Pensioners' Association from the Vicker's workers.

"I'm also a member of the Barrow Working Men's Club. This is quite separate from the Labour Club where the pensioners have their meetings, and I can socialise here, have a drink and a chat and a game of snooker with old friends. There's a real feeling of good fellowship in Barrow's different clubs.

"To round off my story. Neither of my two sons are in Vicker's. The elder is based in Cape Town installing telecom equipment throughout South Africa. He told me some time ago he got an emergency phone call saying they were having trouble with equipment in Windhoak in Namibia. He rang the airport for a flight, 'Sorry sir, all flights booked.' He phoned his office and they said 'Stand by the phone.' A couple of hours later he got a ring, 'Get to the airport. Transport laid on.' It was a six-seater jet that was laid on for him which took him to Windhoak, sixteen hundred miles away, and the work took him just twenty minutes to complete! When he came home last September he and my younger son and daughter-in-law ran in the Glasgow marathon. My younger son and daughter-in-law also ran the London marathon and they are coming up in October to run in a marathon here. My younger son is an air-traffic controller at Prestwick. When Andrew went in, he went in as a pilot. His reviewing officer had been Douglas Bader. He had a lovely session with Sir Douglas. He's one of these blokes who forget the 'Sir.'

"Well, that's the story of the McIntyre's and of my experiences of shipbuilding in Barrow."

ARTHUR PICKTHALL

Ninety-seven Years of Farming

"I am ninety-seven and have been in farming all my life. I remember when I was eight they let me milk a cow into a little beaker I carried around. They had just left enough for me to get something out.

"I was born at Tomcrag Farm near Newby Bridge. Not so long ago I went back on a visit. It isn't a farm now, it's been split up and made into a big house. I lived there with my parents and brother till I was nine years old.

"Tomcrag Farm was about one hundred and fifty acres, mainly stock rearing. At that time, about the end of the century, you didn't keep sheep; there were so many woods about and they didn't want sheep in the woods. We grew hay and only a few potatoes. In those days it was a job making any profit on a farm. If a man had £1,000 he was thought to be very well off. Later in life when I was able to buy Borrans Farm near New Hutton, which my son runs now, it cost me £9,000. Nowadays it would be worth nigh on £300,000. Money values have changed completely during this century.

"My father died when I was three years old. We moved to Sawry when I was nine and when I was ten I worked in a gentleman's house every morning before I went to school where I was lucky to do well.

"When I left school at fourteen I went to work with my uncle who didn't pay me anything. A man on the council said 'You don't want to work with relatives. Get hired on the farms.' I went down to Tower Wood this side of Windermere towards Newby Bridge. As a matter of fact there are two bungalows in the area, on the roadside, each side of a gentleman's lodge. I carted everything it took to build those two bungalows. Stone was quarried out locally and all the other materials I carted from Lakeside Station. I was seventeen then and the farmer I worked for had two horses and carts. I liked nothing better than working with horses. My lifetime ambition was to work with horses.

"My love of horses had started early when we were at Tomcrag. I was carting on the old farm in 1899 when I was eight years old, anytime when I wasn't at school. When my father died, my uncle used to cart wood for wood-cutters. At the end of the year, when they

137

were making charcoal, he used to cart charcoal from the wood to a furnace at Backbarrow. On Saturdays about this time of the year they used to take three horses and carts. There was an old quiet one I could take and I was only eight years old. At that particular time he ran three horses and carts but he couldn't manage three on his own, so I had one and he managed two.

"I worked at Tower Wood till I was eighteen and a half. The farmer took a new place up at Cartmel Fell, but I didn't like that so I got on my push-bike and went to Kendal and I 'stood', as they say, in Kendal to get hired. You stood with the other lads at a certain place. Farmers would come along and have a look at you and see if there was anybody who suited them. It was just like any other market.

"When I went there it turned out to be the wife's father who hired me. He came past me and looked at me, then he asked a couple of men nearby 'Do you know of anyone?' One of the men said 'There's one standing there who looks like doing your job.' That was me. So he turned round and hired me. His daughter had just left school then and it was only about eight years later when I had left that farm that we got married. Her mother had been loath to let me go. she said 'I trust you.' I stayed till their younger son left school; they didn't need me any longer so I moved on. That farm was up near Kirkby Lonsdale. I got experience there of all sorts of farm work, milking and so on.

"They wanted a head horseman down at Middleshaw Hall, a bit nearer Kendal. It was suggested to me that I try for the job. Mr Waller was the boss. He asked me what age I was, I said 'Twenty-one.' He said 'I've never heard a man as young as that for a head horseman.' He asked me 'What wage would you want?' I said 'Sixteen pounds for six months.' He said 'I've never heard such a wage.' Anyway he gave me the job.

"I did all the jobs with horses you have to do on the farm, ploughing, clearing and carting, carrying materials to and from Oxenholme Station and so on. We carted lime from Kendal. Every year there was always a fortnight carting lime from Kendal before the horses were turned out to grass. I had four horses to look after. There was a trap horse, a medium for carting things like turnips, and two big heavy horses for the really heavy work.

"When they were carting lime we got up very early. We'd fodder prepared the night before. There'd be a drink of milk and off we'd go to get the lime. If you didn't get to Kendal early and there were a lot of carts in front of you, the lime used to come down red-hot and it

138

could set fire to the cart. So it was necessary to get there early if you wanted to get the cool lime. A red-hot cinder could set fire to the cart although there was a lot of slack, powdery lime that the man would throw in to keep the red-hot lime from touching the sides of the cart. So it would pay us to get there early. I was at Mr Waller's when the war broke out in 1914. I was at Mr Waller's when I got married in 1919. My wife had never left her family farm, but I had always been in touch with her, we had been friendly for eight years, since she was sixteen.

"I never had anybody to set me up and my money had come out of my own hard work and savings. I didn't want to get married till I had money to support a wife. When at the beginning of my life in farming, and when I was getting £6-10s-0d for six months work, the farmer gave me a £5 note and thirty shillings. I never broke into the £5. The thirty shillings kept me going. Even before that at Graithwaite Estate on the other side of Windermere I did four days pheasant beating at 3/- a day. That gave me 12/-. I bought a pair of shoes for 7/6 and the remaining 4/6 saw me through to Whitsuntide that year. I was fifteen years of age then, when I was doing the beating, I had left school and did the job with a school friend before I started farming. When I got a rise in salary I banked it in the Wakefield and Crewdson's Bank which moved to Kendal and joined up with Liverpool and then with Barclay's. I must be one of the oldest customers in Barclay's.

"As I was getting married I wanted to rent a farm of my own and I got word to say I could rent one on the day I got married. This was Borrans Farm near New Hutton, the farm as I said which my son now runs. I had eight of a family, six girls and two sons, and it's the younger son who farms there. My elder son had a shop in Sedbergh. Two of the girls married into farming.

"When I took over Borrans near New Hutton it was in a very bad state. It was sixty acres inland and seventy acres fell. We were almost self-supporting. We didn't need to buy a lot of feeding stuff for the stock because we had our own grain. I used bone meal through an agent in Kendal. I carted materials from Oxenholme Station and also basic slag. I started with eight milk cows and by the time I gave up I had fifty. My son now, on the same farm, is milking over one hundred and he has added more land to it. I also kept a hundred black-face ewes. The wool off the sheep and the sale of lambs was quite a big part of your income. But you made more out of cows than you did out of sheep.

"In those days you were only selling butter, not milk. We had thirty-five pounds of butter a week at 1/- a pound and that was housekeeping money. Some of the milk was used for feeding calves. We had one customer who used to come for milk. At that time milk was 3d a pint and skimmed milk, milk with the cream taken out was 1d a quart. That was what we used to drink on farms.

"My wife had a full-time job. Thursday was churning day. I hated a Thursday for many times I had to churn for an hour without changing. You couldn't stop churning until the milk broke and curdled. At times you could do it in half an hour, at other times, in cold weather, you could take up to an hour.

"The churn was quite a big barrel. A Kendal firm was noted for their churns. I bought mine second-hand. You often bought things at farm sales when a person was selling out. You went to sales to buy a particular thing you wanted. When you were starting up you bought a lot of things about the farm second-hand, for you had to look after your money. There was a churn you put on a table, the next one was a triangular one with three sides. I can tell you of one old chap on a farm who was let in for churning by the women who bossed him. He hadn't put the lid back properly on the churn. When he was churning, the lid came off and the cream spilled over the floor. He said to the young farm worker 'Quick, give me ma jacket, lad, and let's be goin' before they come and see this lot.'

"In the early days at Borrans I would get up at four o'clock in the morning for I'd work for the council with my horse and cart. It meant doing the farming jobs before I set out on the road with the horse and cart before seven o'clock. I had to carry water for the council's steamroller. It depended on when the council was doing work in your district. It meant at times working for them from seven in the morning till five in the afternoon, but, as I said, that was just at certain times.

"Apart from those times we normally got up at half-past six for the milking. At one time I could do twelve cows in an hour. You got your cows foddered and then went in for your breakfast. You cleaned out the byre and went to work on the land, ploughing or hedging or walling, things like that. Building up broken walls was a continuing job.

"I had a young lad helping me. I had got him from Ulverston which was at that time the best place to find young lads. There were many of them in the Furness area and when things were slack at the shipyard at Barrow, they turned to the farms to get jobs. The young man really had to start learning everything from the start. We had to start milking and, as he got more experience, his wage went up. After two years his wage was getting too much for me and I had to let him go and get somebody else. I was twenty-eight when I started with my farm at Borrans and I was still farming there at seventy when my son took full responsibility for the farm.

"The period from the 1920's till near the Second World War was hard going in farming. About 1930 things were very bad. In 1926 I took three new calf cows to Kendal auction and I got £14 for the lowest and £19 for the highest. Our best lambs only made 17/6d each. Old ewes were only worth 5/-. The railway workers and miners were on stike in 1926. One man I know asked the chap who used to buy the old ewes 'When are you going to give us a bit more for the old ewes?' He replied 'When you get the miners back to work I'll give you a bit more, for they eat the old ewes.' You just couldn't make any money at that time. Even when tractors began to come in at the beginning of the Second World War to do jobs like ploughing, there weren't many farmers who could afford one of their own. A man would go round farms with his tractor and hire out his work.

"During the twenties most milk that was sold was sent to big centres of population like Liverpool. It would be put on trains at Oxenholme. Farmers who lived near a railway station could do it, but most made butter. Farmers would take stuff to the market at Kendal. My wife would take butter and eggs and sell them from a stall. When she couldn't go I would go, but we often went together. It was chiefly butter and eggs we sold, but if we killed a pig we'd make black puddings and we would sell those. We'd kill two pigs each year and we'd sell the hams too.

"In the late thirties, just before the war, the Milk Marketing Board started up and this was the salvation for many small farmers. People started making a little bit of money as milk sales took off. They went in more for milk at that time. You had your milk cheque coming in regularly every month. It in fact was a godsend to those who hadn't sold milk before. So the situation as we approached the Second World War was that farmers were getting a bit more money through the milk and, especially when war started, the increasing use of tractors. Mechanisation was going to revolutionise farming from then on. My eldest son joined the Air Force just before the war started and the youngest lad was only a year old when the war began.

"Sheep dogs have played a good part in the farming life at Borrans. The first dog I ever had was a real good'un. I used to do a little bit of rabbit poaching with it at nights. Keepers got wind of it and one of them laid some poison and poisoned it. I was without a dog for over a year. I had to run with the sheep on the fells. I carried a pocket full of stones and had to throw a stone to turn the sheep. At that time I just couldn't afford to buy a dog. Then I got a dog from a lady and paid only 7/6d for it. She asked me if I knew of anybody who wanted a dog. It wasn't a bad little dog.

"A man that came round the farm let me have a dog. I kept it for a couple of years but it didn't work the sheep all during that time. He wanted me to give him 5/- for it. I said 'You want something for that dog but when are you going to give me something for keeping it for the last couple of years?' It finished up with me giving him half-a-crown and, would you believe it, it started working the sheep next day! That's how I came to have Nell, which turned out a good 'un.

"It's wonderful how you can train a good sheep dog. The very first thing in training a dog is obedience. The first thing was to teach them to sit down, immediate obedience to the word 'sit', and when you whistle, then they stop. When there is a litter of pups there is an old saying, 'Let a dog pick its own.' I let the dog pick its own pup and I drowned the others. Things had to be done in those days. The pup that was picked out was working at six months old. It was one of the cleverest dogs you could have had anywhere. That was Bob, old Bob as he became. I nearly cut its leg off by accident which gave him a limp. I was very upset. I had been using a scythe in a field and there were youngsters around. I said 'Keep well back.' I turned and the dog was behind me. I struck and nearly took its leg off. It healed up not so bad but it always had a limp.

"Bob used to work closely with his mother and nowhere, I think, were there two cleverer dogs. I would set them off round some sheep; they'd look at each other as if to say 'Well, if you're going that way, I'll go this way.' They'd go into a flock and find one out. I'd say 'Watch it!' They'd watch that sheep so it daren't move and I could go and get hold of it. They'd nearly mesmerise it, whichever way the sheep looked, there was a dog. Once I was sorting sheep out for a neighbour. His wife who was watching said 'By gum, you have two good dogs there,' and that was off one I had given half-a-crown for!

"Things improved for me during the war years. When I took the farm over it was in a very bad state and money you made had to go into improving it. Now you were beginning to reap what you had done before. Profit had been a long time in coming, for until then anything you made had to be put back. When you were building stock up you had to balance the books all the time. It was really after the Second World War that I began to make a bit of profit. By that time you were getting a good price for milk and feeding stuff was relatively cheap. Nowadays feeding stuff has gone up and up in price. Big companies supplying agricultural feeding stuff have made a good thing out of this.

"All my life I think I've wanted to be responsible. When I was hired, even at a young age, I was the head man. I had fellows under me and you had to take the lead all the time. Young farmers coming along now think differently from my generation. The paper work has increased beyond belief. In wartime there were forms to fill in. The wife wouldn't have anything to do with that, she'd write letters but she wouldn't fill forms in. Bookkeeping and science are the things now. Calculators and computers are all part of progress.

"I never wanted to do anything but farming, my mind was always set on it. I had wanted to work with horses because I had always got on well with them. I remember one fellow I worked for said 'My horses have never looked better and never cost less.' You've got to know how to handle horses, the good 'uns and the bad 'uns. There are times when you've got to give them a bit of stick, but not often. I think in all my experience I've met only one really bad 'un. That was at Middleshaw. One old chap once said to me about his horses that I was looking after 'By gum, how well they look.' You would almost see your shadow in their shining buttocks. He was poking about in the dung to see what was coming through them. He asked 'What have you been giving them?' I said 'Only what you told me to give them.' He said 'I've never seen now't like it, they're looking so well.' I had been giving them chopped corn sheaves and turnip and a little bit of bran. I fed them at five in the morning and then gave them two hours and they were ready to go to work at seven o'clock. They got the same feed at dinner time, an hour's break and then they were fed again at night - three meals a day. The big Clydesdales were great workers.

"I've seen almost a century of farming. I suppose my life has been the history of farming in Cumbria."

143

BILL GUEST

Sellafield and Nuclear Power

"I was born in Penrith in 1929. My father was a butcher and my grandfather had a shoe shop. My father served his time as a shoemaker with my grandfather and then went into the Army. When he came out, he went into partnership with a fellow called Joe Tindall as a butcher in Penrith. The partnership dissolved and later my father bought a shop in Angel Lane.

"I attended school at Penrith Boys National, but first I went to Robinsons Infant School which is now an Information Centre. Unfortunately my father got blood poisoning very badly which meant he had to stop handling meat. So we moved to Troutbeck and my father bought Troutbeck Hotel in 1939.

"I won a scholarship to go to Keswick School and went there till I was eighteen. I enjoyed living in that part of Cumbria. We had a small farm attached to the hotel and my father, being of the old type, everybody had to work. You had your allotted chores and there was plenty to do at hay time. My mother died of cancer in 1944 and that caused a lot of upheaval in the family and we got a housekeeper.

"I left school in 1949 and just worked at home because I knew I was going to be called up soon. I went into the Army, the Border Regiment at Hadrian's Camp at Carlisle. That was a shocker, the discipline of the Army just after school. Looking back I enjoyed it, for you forget the bad times and remember the good times. After basic training we were sent to Aldershot and trained with the Coldstream Guards.

"When you move in the Army your record precedes you. I was interviewed about my rugby when they heard I had played for the school. I always remember one game we played against the Life Guards. I was five feet nine and these guardsmen were big men who could have picked me up by the back of the neck! When we finished the course I was made Lance Corporal, and then Corporal, and we were sent back to Carlisle. Apparently one of my strong points was drill and I was put on to drilling the new recruits.

"I did this for three months and then they decided to post us again. Some went with the Border Regiment out in Mogadishu, but I was sent to the School of Infantry at Warminster where I was attached to what they called the Support Company, working with mortars, anti-tank guns and so on on Salisbury Plain. I drove lorries, jeeps, Bren carriers. It was very interesting. I enjoyed the goods times and you learned a lot.

"I came out in April 1950. I got my demob. money, the vast sum of £5. By this time you didn't get a civvy suit but were allowed to keep your battle-dress. When I had been at Warminster my C.O., a chap called Collard, had suggested I make a career in the Army. He knew Windermere and he kept pestering me to sign on; he knew I had taken my Higher School Certificate. I played along with him but in the end I decided not to make the Army my career.

"One thing I learned at the very beginning of my Army experience, never to volunteer. What taught me was this: after a fortnight's training the sergeant came along and said 'Can anybody among you drive?' Three of us said yes and he took us along to a coal depot with an enormous heap of coal. 'Right,' he said, 'drive these shovels and keep going till you've cleared it.' That was some job!

"The old man said 'You'll need to get a job now you're out.' I went to the dole office and said 'What have you got?' They said 'We're looking for scientific assistants at a place called Windscale. We don't know much about it.' This was about 1950 when little had been talked about nuclear power. They gave me an address to write to - the Chemical Inspectorate at Kidbrooke. They arranged an interview at Sellafield. They said 'We'll let you know.' Obviously they had to make security checks and so on. By mid-August I got the offer of a job.

"I started on September 7th 1950. I was put in the Chemical Inspectorate as it was then. In those days it was quite different. It was run by the Ministry of Supply, Department of Atomic Energy. The Chemical Inspectorate was separate, it answered to the government chemists at Kidbrooke, it was an independent outfit that did chemical analysis. In the 1950's there was very little to analyse except samples sent up from Harwell to teach us.

"A thorough training course was instituted for us newcomers. There were a few people there, older people who had come from Springfields, some had been at Chalk River in Canada to get experience. For the first four months we were on an induction course which was like being back at school - learning about radio-chemistry, the history and theory of radio-activity and so on, all the training being done at the Sellafield laboratories.

"Sellafield had been built during the war, a Royal Ordnance factory. In 1946 it was closed down and the site sold to Courtaulds, with an rayon-spinning factory on the site. In 1947 the government of the day, it was all secret at the time, decided to build an atomic bomb. They looked around for sites and picked Sellafield as one. The place was taken back from Courtaulds and in 1948 construction work began on two atomic piles and the reprocessing plant. There were some of the old buildings still left.

"When I began in 1950 both reactors had the biological shield and the building round it with the chimneys, one about a third of the way up and the other about two thirds. There were maybe a few hundred working on the site, an awful lot were Irishmen, part of the mobile Ministry of Works labour force, and they were really tough, hard workers. I've never seen people work like them and they were housed in a camp just outside Sellafield. In those days the money they got was very good. We had a look inside the reactors. Now on decommissioning some time in the future, there will be our initials which we carved in the blocks of graphite.

"In 1951 the first pile went critical. In 1952 the second pile went critical. When you run fuel out of a reactor you store it for one hundred days to let it decay. I think it was June 1952 the first radioactive fuel was fed through the separation plant and the first plutonium was produced to explode the bomb in Monte Bello that year. When you think of it, it was quite an achievement, starting from scratch to build a factory with two reactors and a processing plant to produce plutonium in four years, when I think it now takes about ten years just to build a reactor. It had a relatively small workforce, less than a thousand. You knew everybody in it. I enjoyed those days very much.

"During the reprocessing of fuel we wanted in solution about three hundred milligrams per litre of uranium, one third of a gram of uranium per litre. Our job was to analyse samples, to determine the percentage of uranium and the acidity in the samples coming from the plant. We had to ascertain the strengths of different chemicals in the solution, to analyse the fission products to make sure the plant was working as it should, because in the main separation process the first stage of the plant takes out ninety-nine per cent of the fission products and you're left with your uranium and plutonium solution. You separate the uranium from the plutonium and that gives you your two streams. So analysis had to be done on those to see that conditions were right and the strengths of the solutions were right.

"Working with remote control, it wasn't what you see nowadays on television with modern manipulators, we had tongs through lead walls and we looked through glass windows. We were allowed more doses of radiation to the body than is allowed nowadays.

"I had a couple of years on shift, for in those days you didn't volunteer for shift, you were just drafted on. Nowadays you get forty per cent extra salary if you are on shift, but in those days you got nothing extra and our salaries were not terribly good considering the work we were doing - about £30 to £35 a month. That was in the early fifties. You had to pay about £2 a week for the hostel where a cross-section of us lived. Married employees were mostly at Seascale and Egremont and Whitehaven. I lived at the Green Garth Hostel. For transport to the plant I think there were only two motor-cars and a few motor-bikes and push-bikes, so they ran a bus service. The hostel was at Holmrook, about seven miles from Sellafield.

"I was on chemical analysis till 1954, then I moved on to the construction and design of remote control apparatus we built ourselves for other people to use. I worked with a chap called Arthur Hawarth who had very bright ideas that were not always orthodox. As time went on, remote control techniques became more sophisticated. I found it was an advantage to have done chemistry before moving to the realm of engineering. All the time there was quite a bit of research going on alongside the normal analytical chemistry. For instance we built a remote controlled lathe and put it behind a shield so that we could turn pieces of radiated uranium and take off very small slices. We didn't do the analysis. We just provided the material.

"On the engineering side we were always refining our methods and improving our testing apparatus. I had joined a group of engineers and went on into the Engineering Development Group. I was useful here for I knew my way around the site and, if there were any bits of material wanted, I knew where they could be found and could invariably beg and borrow them. In this section I had excellent bosses. One was Bob Catlin. My immediate boss was Reg Clucas who unfortunately dropped down dead during fell-running. The third boss whom I had and remember affectionately was Edmund Strong. As one of my colleagues once said, he was a great lateral thinker, perhaps unorthodox but a super fellow, very very intelligent.

"I was involved in engineering projects. The last one I was in was making plutonium fuel elements. These were for various experiments in reactors to see if they could burn plutonium as a fuel. This was for various experiments for other establishments in the country. That was really, basically, engineering. I worked with engineers all the time even though I wasn't a qualified engineer. A lot of the work depended on common sense assessments and applications. I enjoyed this period which lasted till about 1972.

"During this period we made advances in the use of cameras, and later close-circuit television, to get access to and photograph potentially difficult areas. In one case where we had to get information about what was happening in a vessel where the only access was down a forty foot, four inch tube. At that time my boss was Edmund Strong and we co-operated with experts from Harwell. We devised a periscope which was lowered, so we could look at the area but we wanted good pictures. I suggested getting actual photographs. I remember at the time some people looked at me and said 'What the hell are you on about?' They said 'The film will be black.' I said 'I think we can get down, flash out a few and get back out quickly.' I was given the go-ahead. We settled on a miniature half-frame, thirty-five mil. camera. I see one has just made £2,000 in a sale somewhere. We bought one and had a stainless case made for it and a standard flash gun, then we fastened it to a twenty foot domestic stainless steel piece of pipe and ran wire down. We wound it up so we just had to press it to take a few shots by activating the shutter. We jointed the pipe and put it down. There was no way of seeing what we were doing and we had only thirty seconds to take the pictures before the film would be affected. We knew roughly where we had to point it, so we flashed the pictures and pulled it out. The end result was that we got extremely detailed photographs which showed us how to tackle the problem successfully. That was a satisfactory advance. Then we went on to take stereo photos which helped to show us working areas in better perspective. After photography came close-circuit television.

"We formed a Plant Examination Section where we used all available techniques. Edmund Strong was in charge and two of us were under him. We formed our little section and gathered together our gear. We had got some good pictures inside cells, but by that time we could buy a T.V. camera. Later we could video inside cells and from then on we used video cameras more and more. I got to know quite a lot about them, which came in useful when I retired. We began inspecting the inside of reactors, Calder Hall and Chapelcross reactors, using purpose-built cameras. The emphasis all the time was for greater and greater safety and excellence of production. Everybody was dedicated to that.

"I retired in 1984. Obviously I had always been interested in using video in the factory. I had also done videos of local events. I put them on here and had a few beers and made a little money for the old age pensioners. We would put these on at Bridge Inn, Santon Bridge, where my wife and I have retired. People would turn up and enjoy seeing themselves and we would have a collection. That escalated and I started going round giving shows to different people.

"I had been conned into doing a wedding video once and I thought 'When I retire I'll take this up a bit more,' so I did that for a few years. When I retired my wife Pat was still working. She had been senior tutor of nursing at Whitehaven Hospital. She decided to retire also. So together we went into wedding photography a bit more thoroughly. I used four cameras on this job. We'd be at the church about an hour and a half before a ceremony. I'd set two cameras up remotely at the side of the church and one at the back, then I wandered around with one, a fair coverage.

"I had always been interested in photography, so when Pat retired she bought me a camera which took me into photographs. Now we do colour landscapes. The good ones we get enlarged and sell locally.

"I know there are a lot of people who are naturally fearful of nuclear matters. Perhaps I can speak as somebody who has been literally at the heart of Sellafield from the earliest days. As far as a worker there is concerned, if you obey instructions which are detailed and built up over years of experience, you will come to no harm whatever. Nothing in this world is one hundred per cent safe. When you do a job and fool-proof rules and regulations are laid down for you, if you keep to them, the chances of getting an overdose or contaminated are absolutely minimal. The latest Health and Safety report on Sellafield just out, despite the claims of people like Green Peace that we cut corners, shows independently that this is not so. I have no qualms about that.

"I personally think, if we could get people to differentiate between nuclear weapons and nuclear power, there wouldn't be so much fear and people would accept nuclear power. So many worries are emotional and not based on fact. People are afraid of the effects on posterity, but, should nuclear power be denied, what if our descendants go to switch a light on? There could be no electricity, no energy, no power! What would society do then? For, undeniably, what we call renewable sources of energy which supply part of today's energy, will in the long term run out. There is enough uranium to keep the energy system going for many many thousands of years. The only other use I know for uranium is to colour stained glass windows. So uranium is there for our descendants who will in the future have no coal, gas or oil, but will have uranium.

JOE KEGG

Farm Worker and Miller

"I have been in farming most of my life. When I left school I worked on a farm where I got £5 for six months work. I started at half-past five in the morning and finished about seven o'clock at night. I'd set off delivering milk at half-past six in the morning. I was quite a small boy, just fourteen, and I had to carry five gallon churns of milk upstairs to the still room of a hydro during my delivery where it was used for making the coffee.

"I came to the Crosthwaite area when I was about twenty-one. I was working for John Dixon. My wife's sister and her husband were there. He was farm manager and I lived with them. Through them I met my wife; she came for a holiday with them. I met and married her and we've been married fifty years.

"When I was working on the farm I used to go to George Dickinson's mill down at Cark, near Flookburgh. I used to go to the mill every week for cattle food and I'd take grain from the farm. I'd also go to the mill at Lindale owned by David Chamley. We'd get grain ground up at the mill or rolled. We used to talk about 'sam-ground' or 'sammy', which really meant the grain was semi-ground.

"Money was different then. A farmer could start up on £500. After the third year he could either make a go of it or give up. Still, in those days when money was scarce, I never thought one day I'd have my own mill. I had, up to the Second World War, got a lot of experience on the land. I could do every job about a farm, layering hedges, clipping sheep, looking after horses, ploughing and driving tractors and so on. I'd never thought of doing anything else.

"From just before the war my life started changing from being an ordinary farm worker to something else. I went to work for Mr Craven, in private service as you might say, at Barkbooth. His father was a managing director at Vicker's Armstrong. I looked after his horses, his garden, the electricity supply and so on. In fact I really was his general maintenance man and at that time it was a lift-up from farm work. That was in 1938 and my wife and I were living in a cottage where Jonas Barbar used to live. He was the old clock-maker of Winster. One of his clocks was in what is now called the Mason's

150

Arms at Crosthwaite. We knew the inn then as the Strawberry.

"Just before war broke out Mr Craven said to me, 'If I give you a bungalow, Joe, will you come and live in it?' I said 'Yes.' If the war hadn't broken out I'd possibly have gone to live in that bungalow and might have been living in it still. But things turned out differently. Mr Craven got killed in a road accident in his Rolls Royce and I was conscripted. I was due to go into the Royal Field Artillery, but I was told I wasn't to go to the war, I was to get back to the land. They wanted men with my kind of experience with the land.

"With the end of the war I took up tractor driving for the County Executive in 1946-47, which was the bad winter. I worked eighty-six different farms ploughing with the tractor, all round the Cartmel and Lyth Valley areas and further north. We cut the corn and threshed it. Three of us worked together but I'm the only one of the three still alive. We were working for the Westmorland Royal Agricultural Executive. We were paid by them on contract. That lasted till 1947.

"I started ploughing with the Ferguson tractor. There were only about nine Ferguson tractors in the district. I think I was the best advert for this kind of tractor, for whenever I worked it on a farm the farmer would say, 'As soon as I can get hold of one, I'm having one of those.' It was the first really successful tractor. I had worked with horses on the wheel plough and swing plough and now with this little tractor. I ploughed with it through Cartmel and the Lyth Valley, right the way up to near Langdale. I've ploughed right up on the pass at Blea Tarn. I remember the last time I was coming down from there on the tractor, I had my own motor-bike on the trailer and I had also the plough and cultivator. I thought, 'I'll have to be very careful going downhill.' By the time I got fifty yards from the bottom I was flat out in second gear. Fortunately a gate had been left open and I was able to get right through. I don't think I could have stopped.

"When I was ploughing up in Langdale I used to stop at the Dungeon Ghyl Hotel which Cyril Bulman had. I ploughed for farmers all round the area. At times when I was going round, I would stay on a farm.

"I came in contact with Crosthwaite Mill in 1947. There was a small farm going with it. A man called Norman Buckley who was a motor-boat specialist had bought the mill. He was a solicitor and he knew me through my work with Mr Craven. He bought this mill but he didn't know what to do with it. He came to me and said 'Joe, will you be my manager down at Crosthwaite Mill?' Well, the war work was finishing up, I said 'Yes,' and my wife and I talked it over. Anyway we moved into the house and we bought a few cows and I started work in the mill. The chap who ran the mill before me had more or less let the business go and things had got into a pretty bad state.

"The first job I tackled was the old water-wheel. Then I got the old mill going and I began to make cattle food. I hadn't made oatmeal when I came to the mill at Crosthwaite but I made cattle food, 'sam-ground', pig meal, or whatever farmers wanted. In the beginning I remember there was a chap, Terry Jordan, who used to go around selling feeding stuffs. He had two or three tons of rough linseed cake and asked me to make it into linseed meal, then he mixed it with flour and sold it as calf meal. That was one of the first jobs I did at the mill.

"I built up the mill in about three to four years. Eighty-six different farmers brought in their grain to me, which was oats. It was better fodder in winter than barley straw. I ground it for them and they did their own mixing. I used coke for the kiln for drying the grain.

"There had been a mill on the site since 1328. This one must be about two hundred and fifty years old. I arranged to have it a listed building before I retired. Farmers would drop in on a Sunday sometimes, just for a chat. It was a kind of meeting place and it was great. Sam Hodgson the auctioneer used to come and collect maize for his dogs. His father had started up auctioneering. He'd talk about farm prices and all sorts of farming matters and it was an education listening to him. Old farmers who used to come would get a tot of whisky at Christmas.

"Then one day Mr Buckley, just out of the blue, said to me 'I want to sell, and if you would like to buy it I'd like to sell it to you.' So I managed to buy the mill and land. That would be in 1950 and I bought it for £3,000. Incidentally one of my farmer friends only last week sold a farm for £270,000.

"There are very old documents that tell you about mills in the area. One of them says that in 1390 a man called John de Hall had a fulling mill hereabouts for which he paid a rent of 6/8d a year. About that time a Robert Phillipson paid a dearer price of £2 for the corn mill.

"The corn mill is in the Parish of Crosthwaite and Lyth about five miles west of Kendal. It's inside the National Park. The River Gilpin supplied the water for powering it. The building, as I had it, dates from the eighteenth century with slate roofs and slatestone walls. The mill has a wonderful roof supported by ancient beams. The two drying rooms and kilns are in good condition, as well as the store for the coke and peat. Before I took over the mill, a big water-wheel, ten feet across and five feet wide, had the forty-two iron buckets replaced with buckets made from old Anderson shelters. On the second floor of the mill there's a stone crane, a kind of hoist to feed the grain onto the hopper below. Until I took over, the mill ground mostly oatmeal.

"Just a fortnight after I'd bought the mill a lady from the agricultural people in Kendal, with a sheaf of papers under her arm, looked round the place and condemned the whole lot. After the war they wanted to bring the old farm buildings up to date. I started and did it the hard way, for I did it all myself. I brought everything up to date. I worked night and day, Saturdays and Sundays as well. By the time I'd finished, it was one of the nicest smallholdings in the district, including the mill. I was still grinding in the mill all this time, at the beck and call of eighty odd farmers. It was quite a hard life. Also I used to get peas from Oliver's, the canners in Lincolnshire, and broad beans grown in Lincolnshire by the tulip growers. The roots would go back into the land to provide nitrogen for the tulips. I'd grind the beans into bean meal which was as good as anything you could buy when pigs were still on ration. I'd make barley meal and wheat meal as well.

"I took an agency out and sometimes I'd get five or six tons of Indian corn. I used to grind, kiddle that, and make it into what we called kiddled meals. I got twenty-six shillings a ton, that was for grinding and handling it, the whole lot.

"On the farming side of the smallholding I used to milk about ten to twelve cows, about twenty gallons a day. Looking back on those day I sometimes wonder, 'How did I manage to do it all?' I had pigs too and I used to feed my own calves.

"I kept the mill going till I was sixty when I had to go into hospital. After that I couldn't do heavy lifting. Before that I used to lift ten to twelve tons a day.

"In this area there is probably more sheep coming in with the quotas for milk. When Libby's came into this region, about 1953, things looked good for milk. I remember at that time making stands for the milk churns which would be picked up on a Monday morning. Libby's place was down at Milnthorpe where the milk was cooled and processed and sent by tankers to Leeds, Manchester and so on for human consumption. During the war and later Libby's at Milnthorpe was a creamery.

"In my years of farming I have seen great changes. You might say that over the last two hundred years most farming jobs were done by hand. The really big change came after the war with the use of machinery and science. I've seen twelve horses and carts come to the

153

old mill on a Saturday morning to pick things up. Certainly there were tractors before the war, but farmers couldn't afford to buy them. In fact that was the downfall of some of them, when they did buy one on a loan. They'd get a tractor when they were comparatively flush with money. Then when they were short of money they still had to pay the bank on the tractor, and they hadn't money left to pay what they owed to anyone else. When I asked for my money they didn't like that, and I'd lose a customer that way.

"My wife kept a thousand hens. I was the first in the area to start in deep litter. She looked after these hens and was filling eight thirty-dozen cases of eggs a week. She'd pack them and send them to Express Dairies.

"After my hip operation I was virtually retired, but I still had the mill. It was a big place and there was always some job that could be done. In winter I used to go inside the mill rather than just sit in the house. Say there was a latch on a door that just wasn't right, I'd get a piece of wood; it might take me a day or even two days to cut it properly to match perfectly the old latch. I mended the mill stairs and put a rail up, there hadn't been one before. Jobs like that gave me something to do. During this time my wife took in bed and breakfast guests into the farmhouse. She had a visitors' book with the names of people from all over the world.

"Then about eighteen months ago the solicitor rang me up and asked me about selling the mill. In the end I sold the old mill and the land. My wife and I have now retired to Kendal. I'm still very much involved with the Cameo Club back in Crosthwaite, although when I helped to start it up many years ago it wasn't called the Cameo Club, it was just the village club. At our very first meeting about sixteen people turned up and I was made secretary. The Young Farmers, most of whom knew me, gave us £25. I applied to the Parish Council and I got £50 from them. When the treasurer gave up, my wife took the job on. She had been treasurer of the Women's Institute for twenty-one years. So we've both been involved in the Cameo Club for about fourteen years. When we began to think about a name for the club we didn't want to tie it to any age or section of people, so we finally settled for the Cameo Club. The letters could stand for 'Come and meet each other'. We've had speakers from all over and meetings of all sorts. I organise trips and holidays for the members. Between all that and my garden I've got plenty to do. As a farm worker and miller I've had a busy life, and with my wife a happy one."

ALFRED SIMPKINS

Working with Wool

"In 1909 I was born in Kendal whose motto is 'Wool Is My Bread'. It's the home town of the famous Kendal green. I've worked in the woollen industry all my life.

"My father was a maintenance engineer and worked in the Highgate Mill that folk called Braithwaite's because the Braithwaite family were big shareholders in the firm. At that time Braithwaite's was a weaving mill - weaving, winding, dyeing and finishing, where ninety per cent of the workers were women. They got a discount and could buy cloth at about half a crown a yard. For Westmorland tweeds they used Swaledale wool which commanded a good price, for finer cloth they used merino.

"At that time there were four woollen mills in Kendal: Gandy Mill, Castle Mill, the Highgate Mill where Braithwaite's was before it transferred to Meal Bank, and the Law Mill. They're all gone now.

"Because business in the woollen trade was declining, Braithwaite's closed the mill in Kendal and decided to develop their mill in Meal Bank, owned since 1834. The village, beside the River Mint, was about three miles from Kendal. My father came to Meal Bank and was in charge of all the machinery there. At Meal Bank they did everything - carding, spinning, weaving, winding, dyeing, finishing, everything from the fleece to the finished bales of cloth.

"When we came to Meal Bank in 1921 there would be about a hundred and fifty working in the mill, and that doubled in the next ten years. The mill gave work to most folk in the village. It gave a new lease of life to Meal Bank and it was a busy village for the next thirty years.

"My aunt ran the village shop, just like the village shop in the television series "The High Road" my wife says. It was a small community and there would be about thirty houses. There was no post office but we could buy stamps and things from the postman when he did his rounds. He knew all our affairs and would read the postcards. He'd tell you, 'Your aunt is coming today.'

"The village women worked in the mill and the men folk did any heavy work in scouring, carding, weaving and so on. I started as an engineer and served my general apprenticeship there, getting to know all sides of the business. I got my certificate at the Kendal Technical School.

"Braithwaite's made a great difference at Meal Bank. They did jobs that the council would do nowadays, like keeping roads in good condition. An important thing was getting electricity into the village in 1928, and providing free electricity for the church. The villagers paid 9d a week and 1/3d for upstairs lighting. It wasn't till after the Second World War that meters were installed, the charge was 4/- a month. When electricity came to the mill it cost one penny a unit.

"When we first came the villagers only had paraffin lamps. We had acetylene gas lamps in the mill. Braithwaite's ran two solid-tyre buses every day from Kendal to Meal Bank with about forty passengers each, to take mostly women workers to the village mill. So with its mill, its school of about thirty children and two teachers, and its shop, Meal Bank was quite a busy little place.

"In 1966 when the mill was selling off its houses, one was sold for £180 and another for £250. The whole village could have been sold for £5,000. The average rent had been 3/6d per week.

"As we were so dependent on the River Mint, Braithwaite's had to stop pollution caused by the mill in washing the fleeces, dyeing and so on. They had to take all the dye-stuff out of the water and return it clean to the river. We did this by using chemicals in the water till the heavy stuff dropped to the bottom and the clear water, left on top, went back into the Mint.

"Water and the water-wheel had been the key to all the industrial activities of Meal Bank from the sixteenth century - water from the fast flowing River Mint. If you look across from the opposite side of the river, you see different arches. That's where the tail race came through from the old water-wheels that drove the stones for grinding the corn and oats. The little old mills also produced woollens and snuff.

"A steam-driven steam engine was first put into the woollen mill in 1854, but to start with it was only used when the Mint water wasn't strong enough to drive the big water-wheel. We made improvements in 1924 when we installed water turbines and then diesels. At that time clients were taken round to see our powerhouse which was then very up-to-date. My father supervised all this.

"The villagers got along quite well. Many were on piece-work in Braithwaite's and the rents were quite small. Local girls could buy lengths of cloth cheaply and have them made up. My wife still has skirts and travelling rugs made from the cloth. She made the patterns as well as wove them. The village women would make what we call 'peg rugs' from old clippings. They'd made holes in the hessian and pull them through and level them out.

"When in time I became engineer at the mill I had a lot of dealings with Mr Applegate, who was then the managing director. He came from Bradford-on-Avon in Wiltshire and was managing director at Kendal. He was a great chap and always called me Alfred. Mr Applegate did both designing and travelling around. We'd go up to Shap together; there was a chap up there I knew and Mr Applegate went with me, and he'd buy the full clip from the farm at fourpence ha'penny a pound. We'd make it up at the mill and sell it at Leeds for 2/6d a yard. Herdwick wool was too coarse for our woollen cloth; we used Swaledale wool for our Westmorland tweed and merino for finer cloth.

"The woollen trade began to decline even in the thirties. This was happening all over. I saw it in the woollen mills of the Scottish Borders too. I used to go up to border towns like Hawick and Langholm to the sales of machinery. I saw it happening with our trade in cloth to America when the Americans put an embargo on our exports. A ship would be half-way across the Atlantic when they would put an embargo on because they had had a sufficient quota for the month. The goods were left high and dry and we just had to accept what money we could get for the cloth. When the war came in 1939 things picked up a bit as we were now making uniform cloth and army blankets for government contracts.

"In 1942 I joined the Air Force and did sixteen weeks square-bashing at Arbroath, then duty in Cambridgeshire. My wife, whom I married in 1947, worked on Sunderland flying boats at Troutbeck. Before the war she worked at Goodacres, the carpet factory, in Kendal. Both sides of the family are connected with wool as my wife was a pattern weaver.

"Our mill at Meal Bank closed down in 1966 and three of us decided to go over to Sedburgh and start a woollen mill there. But I had a stroke and had to give up. Mr Applegate died of cancer during the war and my father, who was then a director, and two other men ran the mill after the war. Before the mill closed I had became a director myself. I've had an interesting and busy life in the woollen industry."

ALICE TOMLINSON

Remembering at Ninety

"I was born in 1899 and I've lived a happy life in Kendal. It was a different place from what it is now with all its visitors and their cars, then it was townsfolk and horses. My mother died when I was three and a half. I had aunts and uncles in Kendal. There were five of us and I was the youngest. My sister was ten years older than me and she was thirteen when Mother died, so she was a mother to us. My father married again and I had a step-sister. She was a lovely girl and later emigrated to Australia.

"As I said, Kendal was a much quieter place in these days. Castle Garth where I used to live was a quiet cul-de-sac. As time went on there were fewer horses to be seen and more vans and cars. There was a chap came round to Castle Garth with vegetables with his horse and cart. He had a fruit shop in Allhallows Lane, he used to say to me 'Do you know, this is the coldest street in Kendal.' We'd get the full blast of the wind coming up Castle Garth.

"My brother Jimmy, who was next to me in the family, lived next door to where I lived. He lived with an uncle who owned a shoe shop in the town. When our uncle died, Jimmy inherited the shoe shop. It was at the end of Beezon Road where the tannery was. There's a vast difference there as the old tannery used to be overrun with rats. His shop was at the corner and fortunately he wasn't troubled with the rats, they got more to eat at the tannery than they would have got at his place.

"There weren't repair shops, and not so many shoe shops as there are now, like Briggs, Clarks, Timpson, Manfield. There weren't shops who could do the special work that Jimmy did. He could make strong farmers' boots and repair them and he was in great demand for that. He specialised in farmers' boots. He had had a good training when his uncle was living; because of this he did a good trade and everybody knew Jimmy Tomlinson's boot shop. We had friends among farmers. My cousins had Blackyetts Farm near Crooklands and I used to go out there.

"Jimmy sold ladies and children's shoes too, and repaired them. He was an all-rounder who had gone through the whole trade. He also specialised in ladies Portland shoes. They came from Northamptonshire. They were a wider fitting shoe. Although K Shoes were almost on his doorstep as you might say, he didn't sell them. I don't think he was allowed to sell them. Briggs used to sell for K's.

"One interesting thing, and I'm sure shoe repairers in other parts of the country experienced this, people would come in to get shoes repaired and sometimes they never bothered to collect them. Jimmy would say 'Well, I've kept these long enough, they obviously don't want them.' So after a long time, if anybody came in and saw them and wanted them, he'd let them have them cheaply because, after all, he had already paid for the soling and heeling. It had cost him the material and his time in mending them.

"Nowadays, of course, you don't get so many people having shoes repaired. People on the whole have more money and buy more new shoes, but in those days people came to Jimmy with their boots and shoes for repairing. The farmers and country folk knew he specialised in those strong farmers' boots that turned up at the toes, 'tackety boots' as some folk called them.

"Mind you, there was no real poverty in Kendal, and you didn't see children going round bare footed as you did in some of the big cities early this century.

"From the early days when Kendal was a textile place making woollens, there's been a lot of other industries on the go, and when you think of the farming and the markets you see Kendal hasn't put all its eggs in one basket! I've seen it over the years become a prosperous little town.

"I helped in the shop as well as looking after Jimmy at home when Uncle died, but it was funny because the farmers didn't want me. When they came in they said 'Where's boss?' I said 'Will I not do?' 'No, you don't know what we want. Boss knows.' Of course I knew what was wanted with the women and children. I did the bookkeeping, but I didn't write his letters ordering shoes from different firms. Jimmy insisted on doing those himself and he wrote them just as he would speak, whether there was any grammar in the letter didn't matter. As long as they knew what he wanted, that was the main thing. He was just natural, asking for what was wanted.

"If I'm honest I'd say I spent most time at home and I didn't like the shop so much. I preferred keeping house for my brother at home. Except during the war when everybody was rationed, it was easy to buy what you needed in Kendal. Prices in those days were so much lower. There were the markets, but I didn't use them overmuch, I had my local shops, my butcher and grocer, and got my food there. We hadn't the big stores you see nowadays. The service was very personal.

"I had my brother and cousins in Kendal but they've all gone now. I am the only one left and I live in an Abbeyfield Residential Home. I'm happy living here with my memories of Kendal as it was.

"I learned to drive before the war, my brother taught me. I laugh when I think of it. It was the only time we used to fall out. I suppose it's always the same when families teach each other. Jimmy got his garage built before he got his car and we'd get around the Lakes.

"I got very friendly with the lady who used to come when Auntie was living and help her with her house. Before she died Auntie spent more time in the shop than I did. As I mentioned, the lady came from Stavely, her husband was in poor health and he used to go selling tea from a little van. She would go round helping her husband till he died. She'd come to us on a Thursday morning at half past seven and got a good breakfast and worked till midday - all that for half a crown, and even that was considered to be quite well paid at that time.'

"There wasn't much entertainment. There was St. George's Picture House and they sometimes had dramatic reviews there. It was still going after the war and you could buy season tickets for that. A dramatic society from London took it. I used to go and I enjoyed it. I was a member of the St. Andrew's Society. We had Scottish country dances and Burns suppers and Halloween celebrations. It still flourishes, but at ninety my dancing days are over, I'm too doddery now. When I go to see my nephew Joe who lives in Glasgow, he has to come to collect me in his car. My other nephew lives in London; his father lost an arm in the Cameron Highlanders. Joe's mother was my eldest sister.

"I went to the old Sandes Avenue Church which was later taken down. It was a United Reform church. Now I go to Zion in Highgate, it's called the United Reform. I'm going to a meeting there tonight. I liked the little church in Sandes Avenue and I've made real friends through the church. Altogether my long life in Kendal has been a happy one. It was a simple life of looking after a brother and working in a shop, small scale maybe, but the kind of life that millions of ordinary folk live."